Lost Restaurants

OF

GREENVILLE

Lost Restaurants

OF

GREENVILLE

JOHN M. NOLAN

Foreword by Mayor Knox White

AMERICAN PALATE

Published by American Palate
A Division of The History Press
Charleston, SC
www.historypress.com

Copyright © 2020 by John M. Nolan
All rights reserved

First published 2020

Manufactured in the United States

ISBN 9781467142113

Library of Congress Control Number: 2019956045

Contents

CONTENTS

Foreword

Growing up in Greenville, no one really thought about our city having a "culinary scene." Restaurants were a place to go out for a break from cooking at home or for a special occasion. They were mostly down-home places where you could get a great home-cooked meal in an environment where you often knew the owners or waitstaff by name. Customers around you might be familiar friends, coworkers or neighbors. With the vibrant growth of downtown Greenville, the amount, diversity and quality of choices of places to go out to eat has truly become one of the great facets of our revitalization.

Though certainly not comprehensive, this book represents an important survey of familiar, nostalgic and pioneering restaurants that were the foundation for what we enjoy today. The stories of these immigrants, families, chefs and entrepreneurs are a snapshot of the fabric of Greenville's society for more than a century. The environments they created have been crucial communal spaces for all walks of society to come together and enjoy a great meal.

I hope you will enjoy reminiscing as much as I did as you read and grow in even more appreciation for the people who continue to create great Greenville dining experiences today.

—Mayor Knox White

Preface

When I grew up in the 1970s in Toledo, Ohio, many of my eating-out experiences were in chain restaurants that were near my neighborhood. Places like Frisch's Big Boy, Friendly's and Red Lobster were where we went out to dinner for a special treat. After I moved to Greenville, South Carolina, in 1992, the places I *really* remembered and sought out nostalgically when I returned to Toledo were the one-of-a-kind, mom-and-pop restaurants that offered unique menus and flavors that couldn't be found anywhere else. In Greenville, I longed for just one more Elbo Room pizza, a homemade doughnut from Hinkle's or a Hungarian hot dog from the famous Tony Packo's Café.

Now that I have lived in Greenville for more years than I lived in my hometown, a new crop of restaurants has taken hold in my memories as the locally owned and unique places that I used to love. The first restaurant I tried in Greenville was Capri's on Stone Avenue. The spaghetti was delicious, and the Chianti bottle with melted candle in it and the mini juke box mounted at the table provided a cozy ambiance. I took my family to Ryan's Family Steak House on Laurens Road to fill up my four kids inexpensively but went to Stax's Peppermill only on the occasion of a business dinner (without the kids!). While all of these places are gone now, I long for them one more time just like I do an Elbo Room pizza.

While I personally experienced only about one-fourth of the Greenville restaurants I wrote about for this book, the scores of Greenville natives I've talked to over the years feel strongly about their lifetime of memories eating at so many of these establishments. Their experiences growing up with these restaurants will forever be part of the fabric of their lives. People care deeply about the nostalgic places of their childhoods and love to reminisce about the good ol' days, with places they ate at as primary reference points. This book is meant to preserve the unique stories of these hallowed dining halls for the locals who patronized them but also to give a glimpse of what these restaurants were like for those who were not fortunate enough to experience them.

Speaking with the former owners, their families and customers was a truly wonderful part of this project. Hearing about the work and commitment of these owners to their community brought about a profound new appreciation not only for the legacy of their restaurants but also for the places that are still open and have been faithfully nurturing their neighborhoods for decades. I found myself taking my kids out more frequently to places like the Clock on Wade Hampton, the Carolina Drive-In, Mike & Jeff's BBQ and the Open Hearth to experience these wonderful pillars of our history.

Having worked closely with many of Greenville's current owners, chefs and servers on my culinary tours, my respect for their hard work, dedication and talent has made me greatly appreciate all that goes into making a successful restaurant. Creating an environment that people want to come back to again and again, bringing their children and grandchildren, is quite an accomplishment. While this book captures some of those stories, there are scores of others whose stories are equally compelling and will continue to live on in memories.

Acknowledgements

I am especially grateful for the continuous support and help of Greenville city officials, especially Mayor Knox White; the wonderful team at VisitGreenvilleSC, led by Chris Stone; and the amazing promotion by Taryn Scher at TK PR. I'm also very grateful for faithful promotion by Ariel Habegger Turner, Jamarcus Gaston, Megan Heidleberg Hoffman, Kimberly Kelly, Gabrielle Komorowski, Joe Gagnon, Nicole Livengood, Laura Huff, Stephanie Burnette, Lynn and Cele Seldon, Janice Smith and Lillia Callum-Penso over the years. The following individuals graciously granted me interviews, reviewed the text for accuracy and provided invaluable anecdotes, stories and insights: Kelly Baird, Jeff Bannister, Art Boudoucies, Gina Boulware, George Bybee, Joe Clarke, Tina Berardinelli Colins, Rodney Freidank, Emil Fritz, Steven Devereaux Greene, Reggie Grubbs, Becky Solos Hatch, Leon Kolokithas, Wanda Lowe, John Malik, Steve Perone, Carl Sobocinski, George Stathakis, Carol Stewart, Addy Sulley, Spencer Thomson, Yuri Tsuzuki, Knox White and Lauren Zanardelli.

Thank you to all of the contributors and facilitators (especially Tom Brissey, Jimmy Chandler and Peggy Garrett) of the Facebook sites (Greenville SC Natives, Upstate Past & Present, You Might Be from Greenville, SC If You Remember…, We grew up in Greenville SC in the 50s, 60s and 70s), which are wonderful forums for the exchange of memories of these restaurants and of so many other crucial aspects of city history. I'm also grateful to Kaitlyn Chisholm for reviewing the text.

Acknowledgements

My appreciation for the owners and staff of restaurants has deepened over the years through the close contact I've had with many of them on my culinary tours. It is a hard business. You have to be passionate and committed to make it. I'm profoundly grateful for their work and friendships and for giving my tour guests and me amazing culinary experiences over the years. I'm especially grateful to Michael Abbott, Stacie Amesbury, David Anctil, Sylvia Anders, Elizabeth Anne, Vincenzo Antignani, Pedro Aponte, Andres Arango, Nate Arneson, Chris Arnold, Troy Arnold, Bob Augustyn, Rose Augustyn, Cathy Baker, Charmaine Baker, Matt Ballero, Jorge Barrales Jr., Jorge Barrales Sr., Brian Bautista, Yola Bayne, Jerry Beck, Lindsay Beck, Brandyn Bishop, Jerod Bodi, David Bogle, Spencer Bonezzi, Xavier Bonnafous, Trey Bonnette, Kevin Born, Gina Boulware, Drew Breen, Hannah Bright, Jill Brinson, Kelly Brinson, Justin Brister, David Brock, Savannah Brown, Troy Brown, Jennifer Bryant, Tyler Bryant, Matt Bryson, Larry Bullock, Jason Callaway, Diego Campos, Caleb Cannon, Daniella Cantano, Daniel Cantrell, Tara Cantrell, Ashley Caradonna, Vincent Caradonna, Gina Cardenas, Adrian Carpenter, Ryan Carroll, Bethany Carter, Lynette Carter, Andrea Ciavardini, Kristen Cleveland, Michael Coates, Lena Cole, Jenna Comerford, John Conti, James Conversano, Gerard Cribbin, Brian Crossan, Joe Crossan, Michelle Crossan, Caitlin Cuniff, Emily Dallam, Miranda Darden, Jeff Daugherty, Sybil Davis, Daryll DeBruhl, Crystal Deckert, Jeff Delvechio, Mary Disparano, Sean Dolan, Patrick Dunlap, Trudy Dunn, David Dunning, Kim Eades, DeAna Earl, Kate Edge, Chris Edmonds, Jessica Elvis, Kaitlyn Eppinger, Drew Erickson, Cody Esco, Josh Esco, David Estling, Pam Falvey, Chelsea Farr, Kayley Farr, Joe Fenton, Roxanne Fenton, Catalina Fernandez, Alice Finkelstein, Edgar Flores, Aaron Franklin, Rodney Freidank, Ryan Freidank, Sarah Freidank, Justin Furr, Sarai Garcia, Shaun Garcia, Justin Garner, Samantha Gates, Jerard Gatewood, Chris Gemmill, Christopher George, Kristyn Gizzi, Sebastian Gomez, Zackery Grant, Chet Green, Kimberly Green, Danielle Grigorian, Dan Groppe, Alexandra Santos Hackett, Holly Hamby, Rob Hansen, Luke Haramut, Tania Harris, Alexis Headen, Caleb Henderson, Natalie Hendrick, Lee Hendricks, Sarah Henson, Steven Hernandez, Jennifer Hilberts, Ryan Hileman, Krys Hill, Robert Hodges, Glenda Hollandsworth, Mary Holt, Eli Hughes, Josh Hughes, Sam Hughes, Rob Jansen, Derek Jolly, Ashley Binette Kabel, Cassy Keogan, Kris Kerr, Obediah Kirven, Morgan Knight, Abby Koch, Eva Frye Kolb, Rick Kolb, Matthew Konicek, Leeya Koon, Michael Kramer, Jessica Kuharsky, Craig Kuhns, Emmanuel Legrand, Laure Legrand, Michaela Leitch, Eli Leonard, Jennifer Lewis, Joe (Rudy) Lewis, Cindy Linse, Jeff

Little, Kathleen Little, Brian Long, Shannon Luckie, Jack Lukow, Ray Lyles, Whitney Mabry, Foster Maes, Leah Magouirk, Aimee Maher, John Malik, Travis Mansell, Christine Mansfield, Allison Marie, Tanner Marino, Lauren Martin, Katie Marsh, Amy Mathis, Vince Mathis, Rachel Maurer, Paige Blankenship McConnell, Charles Mcdonald, Andrew McGill, Brian McKenna, Patrick McMahon, Russell Merdjanian, Ryan Miller, Michael Minelli, Randy Monter, Cathy Moore, Charlie Moore, Ashley Morris, Kiara Morris, Ishmel Moss, Bob Munnich, Emily Murray, Sharon Murry, Steven Musolf, Teryi Youngblood Musolf, Olivia Cotton Neary, Ashley Newton, Damion Norton, Jessica Nunez, Katherine O'Leary-Cole, Eric Omick, Tiger O'Rourke, Jose Ortiz, David Owen, Beau Owens, Dre Pawlicki, Joey Pearson, Richard Peck, Bobby Pelligrino, Jason Phillips, Kelly Ann Pitts, Ken Preston, Wayne Preston, Zach Preston, Amanda Ramirez, Amy Ramsey, Camielle Reed, Henry Reinhold, Juan Restrepo, Randell Richards, Guy Ring, Jenifer Rogers, Laura Rodgers, Giovanni Rodriguez, Jake Romano, Donnie Rose, Victoria Moore Rutledge, William Ruwer, Jason Saunders, Nick Simmons, Tyler Smith, Josh Staggs, Ken Talbott, Cody Taplin, Greg Teal, Glenn Thompson, Devon Thurmon, Clark Thurston, Jessica Tollison, Cameron Trieper, Stevie Tucker, Andy Turner, Darrin Turner, Christian Salazar, Sam Saldano, Wilbert Sauceda, Jason Saunders, Whitney Blok Schmidt, Steve Seitz, Brennan Shaak, Haydn Shaak, Mike Shuler, Nick Simmons, Lisa Simons, Darby Smith, Logan Smith, Michel Jones Smith, Steve Smith, Heather Smithgall, Zach Sneed, Kaylee Soluri, David Soper, Allison Spann, Dylan Spencer, Josh Staggs, Candace Kay Stephens, Cindy Stone, TJ Sullivan, Guillermo Tajeda, Cody Taplin, Greg Teal, Jennifer Trammell, Evelyn Truax, Darrin Turner, Jennifer Uphold, Tim Uphold, Leslie Urbina, Brandon Urrego, Alex Vanhook, Jo Vanvick, Daniella Villegas, Becky Walsh, Chris Ward, Todd Warden, Lauren van de Water, Ashely Watson, Chad Wells, Elliott Wells, Bo Wilder, Eddie Wiles, Mike Wiley, David Williams, Chris Willis, Stacey Wingate, Karen Witherington, Jordan Wolfe, Dan Wooley, Ashley Wright, Cheng Yap, Derek Zimmerman and Christopher Zydowicz. To all the chefs, managers and waitstaff not mentioned, I'm equally grateful to you.

The most significant help throughout this whole project has been from my wife, Anne. Without her patience, love and support I could never have succeeded. She and my four children, Connor, Sawyer, Olivia and Maddox, are my daily joy. To God be the glory.

PART I

1900–45: EARLY EATERIES

IN NINETEENTH-CENTURY GREENVILLE, THE CONCEPT OF RESTAURANTS was in its infancy. People ate in their homes and got their meat and proteins from their yards and farms, with supplements coming from local dry good and grocery stores or roadside stands. Reasons for eating out were tied to travel. Hotels like the Mansion House had places to get a meal, boardinghouses and roadside inns typically offered a home-cooked meal and after the railroad came to Greenville in the 1850s, travelers could get food in the station or a store nearby. Greenville's earliest city directory, from 1876, lists just one restaurant. James B. Elkin's boardinghouse and store on Augusta Street across from the Greenville and Columbia railroad depot offered lodging, ale, lager beer, cider, wine, liquors, cigars and a restaurant that was open twenty-four hours. Saloons were plentiful around town, but these male-only establishments primarily served drinks, with a few snacks available. By the end of the century, there were fourteen downtown restaurants clustered on Pendleton Street, Main Street, Broad Street and Washington Street.

As the twentieth century arrived, so did the format of restaurants that would become the standard—a single long counter and tables within the one large dining room. The Gem Café at 118 West Washington and the Occidental Lunch Room at 209 North Main were among the first to appear. Until World War II, the eateries around town were almost all under the titles of café, lunch, sandwich shop or diner. Notable examples are the Blue Ribbon Café at 13 West Washington, Pete's Lunch Room No. 1 at 14 Pendleton Street, Toastee Sandwich Shop at

218a North Main and the DeLuxe Diner at 326 North Main. Soda fountains found at places like Franklin National Soda Shop and Carpenter Bros. Drug Store were extremely popular as well.

As restaurant concepts diversified, tea rooms like Eugenia Duke's, steak houses like Charlie's and barbecue joints like the Barbecue Lodge and Joe Jackson's Restaurant expanded the choices and styles for Greenville's growing population. By the start of World War II, there were about 150 restaurants in Greenville's downtown and surrounding areas, stretching out to places like Augusta Road, Cedar Lane Road and New Buncombe Road. Greenville's Greek community played a dominant role in owning and running many of the early restaurants in town, only a few of which are featured here— Boston Lunch, Charlies' Steak House and the Sanitary Café.

1

Boston Lunch

Owners: Steve Petrakos; Chris, Nick, Spero and George Hassiotis
Years open: 1919–88
Location: 117, 15 and 4 West Coffee Street

When the Boston Lunch restaurant opened in 1919, there weren't very many restaurants in downtown Greenville. One of them was the New York Café on West Coffee Street. Choosing the name "Boston" brought another big-city sense of dining to this small, but growing, southern town. The owner, Steve Petrakos, was born in Sparta, Greece, and his family was one of the first in the Greek community of Greenville.

Very little documentation remains of the restaurant while under its first owner, and no advertisements were published in the newspaper for the forty years that he owned it. Just six years after the restaurant opened, an early-morning fire gutted the interior. According to a *Greenville News* account, the blaze started in the Coffee Street Meat Market and then spread to adjoining Boston Lunch and Greenville Meat Market. The restaurant was fully remodeled, and when it reopened, guests were invited back to enjoy free iced tea or coffee with their meal.

In the 1926 city directory, it had a new address of 15 West Coffee Street. It is difficult to discern if it actually moved locations or if the reason for the address change had to do with the renumbering of all Greenville streets in

BOSTON LUNCH

West Coffee Street

We have remodeled our restaurant and now have room for everybody.

FREE

ICED TEA OR COFFEE

SATURDAY

To Our Friends and Customers.

BE SURE TO COME SATURDAY

Above: Boston Lunch at 15 West Coffee Street. *Courtesy of the Greenville County Historical Society.*

Left: A *Greenville News* advertisement from May 28, 1925, welcoming guests back to the remodeled Boston Lunch after the fire. *Courtesy of the* Greenville News, USA TODAY NETWORK.

1925. Whether or not it moved after the fire in 1925, it did relocate in the early 1950s, across the street to 4 West Coffee Street.

Petrakos, like many in Greenville's Greek community, was a regular financial supporter of efforts to help Greeks in need in their war-torn homeland. Italy invaded Greece in 1940 without initial success, but when Hitler joined forces with Mussolini, many towns and villages were taken over and leveled.

18

The Hassiotis family was one of the many Greek mainland households ravaged by the effects of war. In 1955, after years of rebuilding and trying to make a meager living, Chris and Nick Hassiotis immigrated to America. According to an interview with the *Greenville News*, they first went to Alabama and got jobs cooking in a military officer's club and then later moved to Atlanta to work in a restaurant. They moved farther east to Greenville and bought the Boston Lunch restaurant from Steve Petrakos in 1959. The Greek community that had helped support families like the Hassiotises during the war welcomed them warmly.

Boston Lunch's menu changed little when the Hassiotises took it over. Tasty, home-cooked and inexpensive food is what it was all about. People from all walks of life in downtown's diverse places of work and entertainment came together to enjoy the comfort food. The chili cheeseburger plate and homemade chili were crowd favorites. A variety of sandwiches filled the menu, including fried ham, baked ham, roast beef, roast pork, BLT, ham and cheese, barbecue pork and fried flounder. For a particularly affordable meal, hot dogs and egg and cheese sandwiches fit the bill. If customers wanted to splurge, they could get the club steak, rib-eye steak or T-bone steak. Other meat plates included the hamburger steak (best when ordered "smothered"), Salisbury steak, half chicken or veal cutlets. Seafood options included deep-fried shrimp and flounder. While many restaurants in town had coleslaw, Boston Lunch's was a bit different, with an oil and vinegar base rather than mayonnaise. The Greek salad was the lone nod to their native roots.

A *Greenville News* interview describes how Spiro and George Hassiotis came from Greece to Greenville in the 1960s and eventually joined their brothers, Chris and Nick, in owning and running Boston Lunch. As was often the case in the Greek community, the restaurant grew as a family business, with four brothers and their wives and children involved. George worked the kitchen along with his wife and Spiro's wife. Chris and Spiro worked front of house, taking care of customers and the cash register.

The family worked together, and the regular customers were the extended family who supported the Hassiotises through good economic times and bad. When George died, his son, Gus, took over as a partner, continuing the family tradition. In the early 1970s, when People's National Bank was built and the former five points intersection turned into a pedestrian plaza, the south side of Coffee Street—Boston Lunch's original location—was torn down.

Though Boston Lunch survived many decades of changes in Greenville's downtown, it couldn't stop the changes that came to its doorstep in the

This comparison photo shows Boston Lunch's second location (*left*) with the current view of the building (*right*), occupied in 2019 by Sassafras: A Southern Bistro. *From author's collection.*

1980s. After the Hyatt Regency, U.S. Shelter and other developments brought life to the far-north, commercial end of Main Street, Mayor Bill Workman and the city council extended the efforts farther down the street and toward the center of town.

The next major public intersection after the Hyatt Plaza was at the intersection of Coffee and Main Streets. The newly formed Sister Cities program aligned Greenville with Bergamo, Italy, and an Italian piazza design was the final concept adopted (Piazza Bergamo). The plan called for the corner section of the plaza, where Boston Lunch was located, to be torn down to create a larger public space for the plaza.

The Hassiotises didn't want to move, but after a prolonged, heated stand-off, they were essentially forced out. They ended up with a $190,000 settlement for the takeover. Since the restaurant relied so heavily on pedestrian traffic and the loyalty of regulars who worked downtown, its future was in doubt. Chris Hassiotis invested in a new Boston Lunch near the corner of Pendleton and Academy Streets, but it never gained the vitality of the downtown location.

The Piazza Bergamo plan was never fully realized, and the building was sold to a partnership that promised to renovate the building into apartments and a restaurant (which was also never realized). The many decades of Boston Lunch serving customers home cooking, hospitality and a sense of community are the better memories to hold on to rather than the unfortunate circumstances of its last years.

2

Carpenter Bros. Drug Store

Owners: Bill, Lee, Tom and Walter Carpenter
Years open: 1889–1995
Location: 214, 123 South Main Street

The origins of Carpenter Bros. Drug Store go back to the late 1800s in the first great building for the village of Greenville. In 1823, the Mansion House Hotel was built on the northwest corner of Court Square, the historic center of the city. By the late 1800s, the hotel had helped put Greenville on the map as a favorite getaway for Charlestonians looking to escape the heat of the coast for a few months. The hotel had a long-standing drugstore to serve guests and locals alike. In 1889, Alfred and (John) Lee Carpenter bought out the Mansion House Drug Store and changed the name to A.B & J.L. Carpenter Drug Store. Two other brothers, Tom and Walter, later joined them in the business, and it then became known as the Carpenter Bros. Drug Store.

It didn't take long for locals to appreciate the Carpenters' dedication to their health and well-being, and, consequently, the business prospered. According to historian Henry McKoy, Greenvillians got to experience their first taste of Coca-Cola at Carpenter Bros., and for many years, it was "the only drug store in the state that could purchase the syrup directly from the headquarters in Atlanta." By 1901, there were about a dozen drugstores already selling the drink. According to a *Greenville News* report, one druggist, likely Carpenter Bros., sold twenty thousand glasses that year.

Coca=Cola

TICKETS

REDEEMED,

Bring them in and get a good drink.

CARPENTER BROS.

Druggists and Coca-Colaists.

A *Greenville News-Piedmont* advertisement from 1900 telling customers that they can buy Coca-Cola at Carpenter Bros. Drug Store. *Courtesy of the* Greenville News, USA TODAY NETWORK.

The store remained in this original location until 1924, when the old Mansion House was torn down to make way for the Poinsett Hotel. The store didn't move far. In fact, "Dr. Lee," as Lee Carpenter was affectionately called, could have thrown a prescription bottle from the old location to the new one across the street on the northwest corner of Court Square. A beautiful set of mahogany apothecary cases lined the walls of the new store. A soda fountain and lunch counter were primary attractions, as by the mid-1920s, drinking freshly mixed sodas became the social "thing to do" (and provided a satisfying beverage alternative during the recently enforced Prohibition laws).

Not only was Carpenter Bros. a favorite local spot for lunch, a soda or an ice cream, but it was also the place to get tickets for just about any major sporting event in the area. Locals who were at Meadowbrook Park to see the game where Joe Jackson famously removed his cleats and became known as "Shoeless Joe" would have bought their tickets from Carpenter Bros.

Above: This 1919 postcard shows South Main Street looking north from Court Square with the original location of Carpenter Bros. Drug Store on the left. *Courtesy of the South Carolina Room, Greenville County Library System.*

Left: Generations of Greenvillians remember Carpenter Bros. Drug Store at this location on the northeast corner of Court Square, shown in 2001. *GCL photo by Josh Patterson; courtesy of the South Carolina Room, Greenville County Library System.*

Furman football game tickets were also sold here, as well as passes for the Barnum & Bailey Circus that entertained families for many years.

Greenville mayor Knox White remembers a routine in the 1990s of going across Court Square from city hall to Carpenter Bros. Drug Store nearly every Monday to get a chocolate malt before the city council meeting. It was

Guests enjoy a Greenville History Tours custom culinary tour at the Pickwick Pharmacy and Soda Fountain on Augusta Road. Though the Pickwick also had one of the early soda fountains in Greenville, during a 2007 renovation, it installed the original lunch counter from Carpenter Bros. Drug Store after it closed. *From author's collection.*

about the only option remaining at the time to get a drink in that section of Main Street. There was a group of old timers who always met at the store, sitting around a table and talking about nearly any personal, local, national or world topic that could be discussed. One of their hot buttons was that they were vehemently opposed to two projects Mayor White was set on seeing through. The first project was the renovation of Court Square with new brick pavers, fountains and statues. Fears in the drugstore were that the upheaval of construction would severely hurt their business. The other project they took issue with was the removal of the Camperdown Bridge over the Reedy River Falls. When Mayor White would go to get his malt, he knew he'd have to walk the gauntlet with the group of men making their claims against those decisions. The malt was too good and refreshing to pass up, so he weathered the storm. The Court Square renovation and the Camperdown Bridge removal were ultimately key components in the success of downtown's revitalization.

The drugstore remained in the family for generations, and there were ultimately five locations in the area. Bill and Lewis Carpenter, grandsons of one of the original Carpenter brothers, were the last family owners and sold the building for the attractive offer of $200,000 in 1995. Though primarily a soda fountain with sandwich options, Carpenter Bros. was the only Greenville eatery to ever last more than a century. The legacy of the old store fortunately lives on, as the old apothecary cases have survived several other businesses that have occupied the space since the drugstore closed. Also, locals can still enjoy the actual soda fountain and lunch counter seating in their restored state at the Pickwick Pharmacy on Augusta Street—another great family-owned pharmacy with its own soda fountain/lunch counter legacy.

3

Charlie's Steak House

Owners: Charlie, Paul, Peter and Kay Efstration
Years open: 1921–2014
Location: 111 West Coffee Street; 18 East Coffee Street

Charlie Efstration, namesake for Charlie's Steak House, was born in 1891 and came to the United States from Smyrna, Asia Minor (now Izmir, Turkey), in 1910. After some time in New York, Efstration traveled to several cities in the South. In a 1963 interview with Elizabeth Stipp of the *Greenville News*, he recalled his first venture into the restaurant business, when he and two friends opened an establishment in Oklahoma. He said, "when a Greek meets a Greek, they open up a restaurant." This was just the first of four short-lived attempts at making it in this difficult vocation. His first real success came with his fifth restaurant, which he set up in San Angelo, Texas. It was here that he developed a deep firsthand knowledge of cattle and how to cook a great steak. Health issues forced him to seek a more temperate place to live, and he settled in Greenville, South Carolina, in 1921. It was a great time to move to the city, as the local economy was booming from a successful textile industry.

It didn't take long for Charlie to continue his passion for hospitality and serving up great food. He bought out the old Capitol Restaurant at 111 West Coffee Street and built his reputation with his wife, Catina, at his side. In 1934, he moved his restaurant to the iconic location at 18 East Coffee

Street, where it would remain for the next eighty years. His time in Texas gave him just the right contacts and insights he needed to bring quality meat to Greenville—and to cook steaks to perfection. The extra-large porterhouse T-bone steak and rib eye were particular specialties. Veal, chicken, pork chops, spaghetti and seafood dishes were other favorite options. He also developed his own special recipe steak sauce and house-made salad dressings that customers raved about. Charlie was active daily, greeting people and cooking in the restaurant.

In 1946, renovations added more space to accommodate more than two hundred guests. Typical for a Greek-run restaurant, the business was a family affair. Charlie's sons, Peter and Paul, were honorably discharged from the armed forces and returned to Greenville to assist in the daily management and kitchen work of the operation.

By the 1960s, Greenville's historic textile industry was beginning to head oversea for cheap labor. The economy of Greenville was hit, but in 1965, hope remained with the building of a twenty-five-story skyscraper as the new corporate headquarters for Daniel Construction Company. That same

This 1946 advertisement in the *Greenville News-Piedmont* announces the reopening of Charlie's after a major renovation. Pictured along with Charlie (*upper left*) are his sons, Paul and Peter, who returned from the war and helped run the restaurant for more than a half century. *Courtesy of the* Greenville News, USA TODAY NETWORK.

Right: The exterior of Charlie's after the 1946 renovation. *Courtesy of the Greenville County Historical Society.*

Below: The interior of Charlie's after the 1946 renovation. *Courtesy of the Greenville County Historical Society.*

A GREENVILLE
LANDMARK SINCE
1921

Charlie's Steak House is the oldest restaurant under the same management in Greenville . . . Native Greenvillians and visitors alike know about the fine food and service that Mr. Charlie offers them.

REDECORATED FOR YOUR DINING
PLEASURE

Mr. Charlie Efstration and his family are proud to be a part of Greenville . . . Earlier this year he showed that he had faith in the economic prosperity of Greenville, by completely remodeling his restaurant both inside and out . . . Nothing has been spared to offer you the very finest in dining pleasure

CHOICE STEAKS

ESPECIALLY PREPARED TO YOUR LIKING
THE BEST AT SUCH A MODERATE PRICE

Charlie's
STEAK HOUSE

18 E. COFFEE ST.   CE 2-9541

WE HONOR
• AMERICAN EXPRESS
• CARTE BLANCHE
• DINERS' CREDIT CARDS

MR. CHARLIE

In 1965, Charlie's underwent another major renovation of both the interior and exterior, as announced in this newspaper advertisement. This would be the look and décor that remained until the restaurant's closing. *Courtesy of the Greenville News,* USA TODAY NETWORK.

year, Charlie showed his continued commitment to downtown with a full renovation of the exterior and interior of his restaurant. Changes included new wall paneling and fixtures and a new English tavern motif entrance with stucco and wood beams around the doorway. This décor is what largely remained in place over the coming decades.

Charlie died just two years after the big renovation, and his capable sons maintained the restaurant. The coming decade was difficult as department stores and regular customers left for the suburbs. On East Coffee Street, the Corner Pocket and Never on Sunday were the only restaurants besides Charlie's Steak House to weather the downturn.

Eventually, Paul's daughter, Kay Efstration, took over the family business. As a little girl she grew up refilling guests' iced tea. She pursued another career but came back when her father's health waned and someone was needed to carry on the family (and Greenville) tradition.

In the 1990s and 2000s, the revitalization of Greenville's downtown brought new restaurants all over Main Street. Charlie's remained a place where generations of locals could continue to enjoy a familiar space that recalled a time gone by and enjoy a consistently great steak dinner. In 2014, with no one in the family to take over the restaurant, Kay decided to close. In one of the toughest businesses for longevity, Charlie's was the oldest continuously running family restaurant in South Carolina history when it closed.

4
Duke Tea Room at the Ottaray Hotel

Owner: Eugenia Duke
Years open: 1918–20
Location: 300 North Main Street

The coming of the Ottaray Hotel to North Main Street in 1909 was a momentous occasion for Greenville. Not since the Mansion House was built at Court Square in the 1820s had a hotel with such grandeur, presence and elegance graced Main Street. Nearly a century after Greenville's first great hotel was built, the city could now boast its new elegant and architecturally unique hotel. The hotel sat at the highest point in the city on the northeast corner of North Main and Oak Streets at the end of a residential section of town lined with big Victorian homes.

The distinctive architecture boasted a stately semicircular balcony supported by four two-story columns. The balcony connected the two five-story brick wings and provided what would be the most coveted, socially relaxing place in town. Guests and residents alike eased into the many wooden rocking chairs to chat, gossip, watch the attraction of automobiles going down the street and get a clear bird's-eye view, looking south at Main Street. An elegant dining room served locals and guests hearty breakfast, lunch and dinner meals.

While it took the Ottaray about a decade to get a solid, high-standing reputation throughout the South, it took only a few years for a local

Ottaray Hotel, Greenville, S. C.

The Ottaray Hotel was built in 1909 at the edge of downtown on North Main Street and was the grandest hotel in town. The Duke Tea Room was located just to the right of the entrance. *From author's collection.*

Greenville woman to gain the same level of notoriety. Mrs. Eugenia Duke was an ordinary Greenville mother who loved to cook. What was unusual was the unique taste of her homemade mayonnaise. Her recipe was thought up and perfected in her house on Manly Street near downtown Greenville and was suitable for keeping indefinitely in a can or jar. In 1917, this "kitchen chemist," as she called herself, began a little cottage industry making pimento cheese, chicken salad and ham salad sandwiches in her home and delivering them to places where locals could buy them. The same year she began her business, a World War I army base, Camp Sevier, was built across town. More than thirty thousand soldiers were stationed there, and they couldn't get enough of Mrs. Duke's delicious sandwiches.

In 1918, with the business in full swing, Mrs. Duke partnered with the prominent Ottaray Hotel and opened the Duke Tea Room inside its elegant walls. As proprietor, Mrs. Duke established a great reputation for serving delicious delicacies and dainty sandwiches. The taste of her famous mayonnaise could now be enjoyed on a daily basis and could be exposed to the masses in a prominent location. Sunday dinners were a popular choice when people could have such delectable choices as fried chicken, turkey or English pheasant. Holiday meals spent at the Duke Tea Room were special occasions, where for $1.50, a guest could have a Christmas dinner plate with roast turkey, steamed rice, creamed potatoes, peas, sweet potatoes, hot rolls and more. The feast could be topped off with a delicious slide of Duke's Homemade Cake.

The restaurant lasted only about two years, though. As regional demand grew for her mayonnaise, Eugenia decided to sell the operation and focus her full attention on the sale of her popular condiment. This hardworking

Above: A 1920s postcard showing a Duke's delivery truck on Main Street. *Courtesy of the South Carolina Room, Greenville County Library System.*

Left: A 1919 advertisement in the *Greenville News-Piedmont* announces some of Mrs. Duke's savory Sunday dinner options. *Courtesy of the* Greenville News, USA TODAY NETWORK.

woman wore most of the hats for her company—president, general manager, superintendent and auditor, as well as being on constant duty as a traveling salesperson and speaker. Within a few years of selling her restaurant, demand had grown so much that Mrs. Duke rehabilitated the old 1904 Greenville Coach Factory paint shop along the Reedy River and opened her first large-scale mayonnaise operation.

Duke's Sandwich Shop still operates at several locations, while Duke's mayonnaise was sold to C.F. Sauer Co. in 1929 but still operates under the name that made the product famous.

In 1955, a larger Duke's plant was built just off Laurens Road in Mauldin to take on the increasing production demands, which became so great that the plant has expanded at least seven times. The modern facility is well over 300,000 square feet—a far cry from its modest beginnings in this charming building on the edge of the river. Today, Duke's is still a guarded recipe and is the only large mayonnaise company to use only yolks (no egg whites) and is sugar free. The Mauldin facility remains the sole producer of the South's favorite sandwich spread, and the original factory on the banks of the Reedy is now named the Wyche Pavilion.

Fall Street Café (The Cat Dive)

Owners: Noah "Noey" Lowe and Noah "Rick" Lowe Jr.
Years open: 1932–97
Location: 401 Falls Street

When Noah Lowe was born in 1890 in Toxaway, North Carolina, the textile industry was well on its way to becoming one of the biggest economic and job engines in the South. Greenville, South Carolina, had a lot of mills opening by the turn of the century, so Lowe moved there (161 Cleveland Street) with his mother and sister around 1912. He was a machinist and his sister, Artie, got a job at the Camperdown Mill. The Camperdown Mill No. 1 and No. 2 were the first mills in downtown Greenville using the power of the river's two waterfalls. After working as a mechanic in Cooper's Garage, Lowe secured a job as a steamfitter serving the pipework of the mills.

By September 1929, Greenville mills were slowing production and alternating weeks of operation or only working three-day weeks. A year later, the Red Cross appealed to local bakeries for day-old bread to feed the hungry amid unsurpassed relief demands of the Great Depression. From his house, Noah could see the impressive chamber of commerce building on Main and East Court Streets, which was the first "skyscraper" in town when it opened in 1925. The chamber couldn't pay its bills and was sold to an insurance company in December 1931. A month later, the People's State Bank closed and was predicted to pay its patrons only 18

Exterior view of the Fall Street Café. *Courtesy of the Camperdown Mill Historical Society.*

Postcard showing Camperdown Mill No. 2 (*left*) and Camperdown Mill No.1 (*right*) seen from the newly constructed Main Street bridge. *From author's collection.*

percent of their savings. A woodyard on East Broad Street was one of the few employment opportunities in the early 1930s. Even though it was right around the corner from his home, Noah was unable to secure a job there and was unemployed.

Perhaps when Franklin Delano Roosevelt stopped in Greenville in May 1932 and told the crowd, "As I see it, the prospects are extremely bright for a Democratic administration at Washington during the next four years," Noah gained the determination to open a storefront directly across the street from the Camperdown Mill. It was a simple operation, selling items like ice and hot dogs to make enough money to feed his family. Though officially he named it the Falls Street Café, a mistake in the spelling of an early storefront sign, reading "Fall Street Café," determined the name people would know it as. Soon, though, the restaurant would be referred to by another name, the Cat Dive. This nickname came from an advertisement of the Cat's Paw brand of rubber heels for shoes on the side of the building. The artwork depicted a cat diving into a heel, and the name association began.

This dive was a true, small, no-frills place for locals to gather for a short-order meal. These locals were mill hill workers from the surrounding Camperdown Mill village. If you came in and were not from the village, you'd stick out like a sore thumb. Everyone knew everyone who ate there. Folks on the go to their nearby jobs could sit at one of the five bar stools to enjoy a stack of pancakes or eggs in the morning. Coffee served in an old urn was flowing all day. Those wanting the option to linger longer to chat could choose from one of the five booths or one larger table that could seat six. That was the capacity.

The lunch and dinner menus were as simple as the breakfast staples and remained nearly unchanged throughout its history. Hamburgers, fish steaks, French fries, beans and hot dogs were the primary features—the ultimate inexpensive comfort foods of the twentieth century in the United States. Depression-era mill villagers needed cheap, filling food, and hot dogs were by far the most popular items sold. Cat Dive hot dogs served at pennies apiece would rise to iconic status, and most were served "all the way," with onions, mustard and a homemade chili sauce with a unique recipe and flavor. The other dish that became a favorite was the hamburger steak smothered in gravy and cooked onions. It was called the "70" because in the early days, the meal cost $0.70 and came with tea. Though the price rose a bit over the years, it continued to be referred to by regulars as the 70.

By the 1950s, Japan had become an international powerhouse for production of ginghams and other fancy textiles (the Japanese TNS Mills came to South Carolina in the next decade under Kiyohiri Tsuzuki, future owner of the Seven Oaks and Nippon Center Yagoto restaurants). The Camperdown Mill was South Carolina's first victim of the overseas competition, and it closed in 1956. For the village millworkers and the Cat Dive, this was devastating. Not only did the mill close, but after a few years, much of the village, including the Methodist church on Choice Street, was also razed to make way for the new Church Street overpass that would bisect the community. The adjacent Reedy River Falls were heavily polluted and overgrown, so the Camperdown bridge was erected in 1960 to allow traffic to easily pass over the river to the West End. Noah Lowe feared it might be the doom of his business.

The Cat Dive remained a stalwart amidst the change going on all around it. With less of a mill village customer base, the restaurant continued to get a steady stream of daily employees from the *Greenville News* production plant across the street (which greatly expanded in the mid-1960s) and the new C & S Bank built on the former site of the Camperdown Mill.

In 1962, Rick Lowe took over the business. Rick had helped out at the restaurant all his life. It's what he knew, and the customers knew him. His right-hand man for the next three decades was Roy Bagwell. Hot dogs were still sold for five cents each, or six for twenty-five cents, and hamburgers were eight cents. With deals like this, business actually grew in the years following the mill closure.

Rick opened at 3:00 a.m. and stayed open until late at night, serving people who worked any shift at the nearby police station, newspaper, bank, Duke Power and other downtown office buildings. *Greenville News* employee Reese Fant was a regular. He started coming to the Cat Dive in 1968 and ate lunch there nearly every workday for thirty years, seated at the third bar stool from the left. In a *Greenville News* article, Fant recalled, "Rick and I solved the world's problems."

Rick would frequently hear about some juicy news or insights and would tell the patron to wait around until Fant got there so he could get the inside scoop. "No telling how many good stories that ran in the *Greenville News* came from those conversations," said Fant. Shoeless Joe Jackson was a customer there, too, and Fant fondly remembers one day when Joe actually let him briefly wear his 1919 World Series ring.

In 1966, Dan Goodwin, a regular, and his friend stopped in for lunch at the Cat Dive and got wrapped up playing pinball in the back room.

A photo from the Cat Dive's last day of service showing longtime employee Roy Bagwell. *Courtesy of Tony Earnest.*

They kept winning free games and kept playing. That was no ordinary day, though. After getting caught up in winning, Goodwin suddenly left in a flash and recalls, "I was almost late for my wedding that day!" The stories abound. Another regular, Tom Brissey, had a family-run repair garage on East Broad Street and ate lunch at the Cat Dive about six days a week and played hundreds of games of pool in the back room. Bill Gosnell took his girlfriend Trudy there for their first date, and they were later married and continued to go back to the Cat Dive until it closed.

Rick's daughter Wanda remembers that her dad had a piece of paper taped to the wall with people's names who needed to borrow money. Rick obliged and scratched off names as they made good on their promises to pay. As the 1960s ended, Rick still opened early in the morning but closed at 4:00 p.m. and only served Monday through Friday.

Fall Street Café continued to be the go-to, no-frills dive that attracted people from all strata of Greenville society. Guests filled up on good food in a well-known environment with familiar people. In 1997, Rick was getting up in age and shared the news that the restaurant would be sold and torn down. People packed the place for weeks leading up to its closing to get their last tastes of those "all the way" hot dogs.

Rick went on to work for the City of Greenville as a parking attendant before finally retiring. While Rick was still alive in 2007, an event called

Back to the Cat Dive was created for the Camperdown Mills Historical Society. Rick contributed the meat and cooked the chili for the fundraiser. The centerpiece of the event was service of the hot dogs with Rick's secret chili sauce that people enjoyed for so much of their lives. When he was no longer able to help, he gave the society the recipe and permission to continue the lunch. The get-together continued to be such a success that as of the writing of this book, the event is still held annually in May in the fellowship hall of St. Paul's—the only original church left from the Camperdown Mill village.

6

The Sanitary Café

Owners: James Gares; George Boudoucies, Pete Bybee and Frank Solas;
   Bill George and Frank Bobotis
Years open: 1919–77
Location: 118 (changed to 20) and 17 West Washington Street

In the years before coming to Greenville, James Gares was known as one of the leading Greek citizens in Charlotte, North Carolina. He had a successful confectionary called the Candy Kitchen inside the Piedmont Theater building. In March 1919, he sold the candy business and opened a restaurant called the Sanitary Lunch in the same building. Soon after, James and his brother came to Greenville to open a similar concept. In their opening announcement for the Sanitary Café at 118 West Washington Street, they said, "This café is to be something entirely new for Greenville, but the soundness of the idea has already been demonstrated as anybody who is familiar with the Sanitary Café in Charlotte will tell you."

However, the Gares's Charlotte store only lasted a few months before it folded, and they moved to Greenville. Nonetheless, the cleanliness for which they strived would be on a level that, perhaps, *was* new. They promised, "Everything will be subject to public inspection and we are sure there are many people [who] have been wishing for such a place as we have opened." The modern-day, open-kitchen concept made its first Greenville appearance here, as all food was prepared and served in full view of the customers.

The Budweiser Clydesdale horses coming down Washington Street with the Sanitary Café in the background. *Courtesy of George Bybee.*

A few days after opening, the Gares brothers ran another ad in the *Greenville News* for their first Sunday dinner, stating, "We have had many compliments paid us on our cooking. Our service is unsurpassed and the cleanliness of everything in our establishment, and having everything in full view of the public has convinced all who have been to our place that we are indeed… The Sanitary Café." Within six weeks, the restaurant enjoyed "more than liberal patronage," and the brothers decided to show their gratitude by hosting a dinner of appreciation on August 10, offering a half-off special Sunday dinner.

Apparently, the Sanitary's new concept put pressure on the nearby competition. Within weeks of its opening, the Royal Restaurant a few doors down began advertising, "Visitors always welcome to inspect or sanitary kitchen," which was not open to public view. The Astor Lunch a block down the street closed for a week in November for remodeling so it could claim it "will be one of the most sanitary cafes in town."

For reasons as yet unknown, James Gares sold the restaurant on December 7—just five months after opening. A *Greenville News* notice on January 10, 1920, said that transaction was "by James Gaies [*sic*] to George Peletis and partners." Given that *Greenville News* reports never spelled James Gares's name correctly in articles written at the beginning or end of his ownership,

GOOD NEWS!

The Sanitary Cafe is Ready for Business

We are today opening a Sanitary Cafe on the first floor of the Wallace building. This cafe is to be something entirely new for Greenville, but the soundness of the idea has already been demonstrated as anybody who is familiar with the SANITARY CAFE in Charlotte will tell you. Mr. Gares and Mr. Michael, who have only recently sold the SANITARY CAFE in Charlotte, will be personally in charge here.

The name of the cafe is to be lived up to and there will be a sign on the front door reading "no flies allowed in here."

Everything will be subject to public inspection and we are sure there are many people who have been wishing for such a place as we have opened.

Prices will be moderate. You can get anything from the simplest meal to the most elaborate spread.

We invite you to come in and look around and we are satisfied you will be pleased.

THE SANITARY CAFE
First Floor Wallace Building

An announcement on July 4, 1919, for the opening of the Sanitary Café on the first level of the Wallace Building. *Courtesy of the* Greenville News, USA TODAY NETWORK.

it is likely that they also misidentified the buyer's, which likely was George Boudoucies and partners. The partners referred to would have been Pete Bybee and Frank Solas.

According to George Boudoucies's son, Arthur, all three of these men came to Greenville together from Fort Lee, Virginia, and got into the restaurant business. In interviews with family members of Pete Bybee, Frank Solas and George Boudoucies, all have recollections that the three were partners from the earliest days of the restaurant. Furthermore, subsequent newspaper interviews with the three owners themselves reveal that they were involved since the origins of the business. As further support, no mention of a George Peletis is ever made in the *Greenville News* before or after the January 10, 1920 notice. Whether or not the three friends worked at the Sanitary before Gares sold it, they seem to have taken co-ownership on December 7, 1919.

By late 1919, the downtown Greenville food scene was up and coming. The city population was about twenty thousand, and when the area millworkers were added, that number doubled. Though Camp Sevier had moved out by then, Mrs. Eugenia Duke's mayonnaise production was thriving, and she had just opened Duke Tea Room at the Ottaray Hotel a year earlier. Of the twenty-eight restaurants located downtown that year, almost half of them were clustered on either Washington Street or Coffee Street. Washington Street had the heaviest competition, with the likes of the Royal Restaurant, Astor Lunch, Eagle Lunch, Gem Lunch Room, the New York Café and Boston Lunch (which also opened in 1919) only a few buildings away.

As Boudoucies, Solas and Bybee were getting to know their customers that year, surely one of the hottest local topics of discussion would have been local boy Shoeless Joe Jackson's scandalous World Series and subsequent banishment from professional baseball. Prohibition would have been another hot topic as the restaurant's first year came to a close and the amendment was put into effect in early 1920. While not being able to sell alcohol put a strain on restaurants, it also led to families taking children out to eat for the same reason—an alcohol-free environment. Bootlegging moonshine in the northern "dark corner" part of Greenville County would soon become infamous.

One of the big factors contributing to the initial success of the Sanitary was its proximity to the trolley line that passed in front of its doors throughout the day going to the train station at the end of Washington Street. In those days, train stations were integral parts of everyday life. Big street clocks, like the one around the corner from the Sanitary in front of Hale's Jewelers, kept passengers abreast so they wouldn't miss an appointment. Living along the trolley line was a big convenience and having a business on it helped bring a regular stream of customers.

The other major factor helping to secure the customer base of the Sanitary was being a few blocks away from the newly built Textile Hall. In May 1919, the hall hosted the third Southern Textile Exposition. It was one of the largest events in the South and brought around thirty thousand people to town. A month later, a fashion show and large automobile show brought more crowds. These were followed by more bookings, including a regional Southern Baptist meeting and the first reunion for the Thirtieth Army Division veterans who trained at Camp Sevier.

The Roaring Twenties were good years for Greenville and for the Sanitary. Downtown was rapidly being built up with office buildings, shops and restaurants. People considered the Sanitary "the most popular café in town," and it was the only twenty-four-seven restaurant to be found. According to Arthur Boudoucies, his father, George, was the chef and managed all aspects of the food preparation, including cooking, baking and butchering the meat.

He would start his workday at 6:00 a.m., serving the breakfast crowd who were fueling up for their workdays. George cooked only fresh eggs that had had been laid the day before and brought in from the farm. Guests could get two eggs with grits, toast, jelly and butter for just $0.35. Coffee was bought from the National Simpson Coffee Co. on McDaniel Avenue and was freshly roasted. For lunch, George's roast beef, turkey and chicken dishes were favorites, with meats coming from the local Balentine Packing Co.

The morning and afternoon shifts were when Pete Bybee worked the front of house, greeting guests, seating them and working the cash register. Baseball would be a common subject for Pete, as he was a co-owner of the Greenville Spinners minor league baseball team.

After feeding the lunch crowds and prepping for supper, George went home around 4:00 p.m. for a two-hour break. When George came back to cook for the evening guests, Frank Solas would take his shift and work into the early morning. Surely a topic of discussion when Frank worked was the stories of being neighbors with Dr. Albert Einstein's son Hans on Randall Street. Hans moved in four doors down from Frank in the late 1930s. The whole city was abuzz when Hans's famous father visited in April 1941, while also guest lecturing at Furman University. All of the local cafés and lunch counters must have lit up with talk of who got to see or hear him.

Postcard showing the interior of the Sanitary Café at 20 West Washington Street—its second location. *From author's collection.*

Portrait of Frank Solas, one of the longtime owners of the Sanitary Café. *Courtesy of Becky Solas Hatch.*

Supper included hickory charbroiled western prime steaks, roasted leg of lamb, calf livers, veal and pork tenderloin. For several decades, the waiter who would have most likely served you was William Theodore, affectionately known to regulars as "Mr. William." A *Greenville News* article about him stated that "he can take orders from dozens of persons at the dinner party (even if it includes some exceedingly specific instructions to the cook), or even scattered at booths and tables throughout the restaurant, serve each person promptly, then stand at the cash register and collect each bill correctly—all without use of his order book. For nineteen years Mr. William has worked at the Sanitary Café on West Washington Street, where he has become a permanent installation, almost a tradition."

The long-standing spot on the north side of West Washington Street came to a close in 1953, when the neighboring F.W. Woolworth Co. planned its expansion into the old Wallace Building space. However, patrons didn't need to go far, as the Sanitary was able to secure a location directly across the street at 17 West Washington. A big celebration took place for the grand opening of the new facility, and crowds came in to admire the new and modern features, the larger dining space and the private dining Plantation Room with service up to one hundred guests. Free coffee, ice-cream and cake encouraged people to linger that day but what kept them coming back was the familiar hospitality and home-cooked food of the team of George, Pete and Frank. They served up favorites like their famous roast beef and steaks but advertised "finer and tastier foods than ever before," with an extensive seafood menu including oysters on the half shell, live Maine lobsters, jumbo shrimp, clams in the half shell and Florida lobsters. In the 1950s, the increasingly popular meat and three dinners for $0.75 complimented the appeal to families to dine with their children.

The 1950s were great years for the Sanitary, with a steady stream of business. By the end of the decade, however, the dynamics of Greenville began to change. People were moving farther into the suburbs. Pleasantburg,

SUNDAY DINNER

FRIED CHICKEN, 3 VEGE-TABLES, DRINK, DESSERT $1.00

SANITARY CAFE

20 W. WASHINGTON
"The Place of Distinction"

In a 1957 advertisement, the Sanitary was appealing to families with children to enjoy their Sunday dinners. At one dollar for a meat-and-three, it was an attractive proposition. *Courtesy of the* Greenville News, USA TODAY NETWORK.

Augusta, White Horse and Wade Hampton were major roads leading into town that saw an explosion of growth along their curbs. One of the Sanitary's later partners, T.C. Theodorou, pursued the opportunities on Augusta Road by opening the Charcoal Steak House in 1958.

The popularity of outlying places like the Charcoal House, Vince Perone's, Ye Olde Fireplace and the Open Hearth began to erode the viability of downtown restaurants in the coming decades. The exodus of downtown department stores in those same decades also meant fewer regular customers for places like the Sanitary by the 1960s and '70s. After almost fifty years of running one of Greenville's finest downtown restaurants, George, Pete and Frank decided to retire and sell the business to Bill George and Frank Bobotis. The pair were familiar within the Greek community and with the restaurant. Even though they continued to offer the popular meat and three specials twenty-four-seven, the decline of downtown's vitality and safety were growing problems for all businesses.

In 1977, Al Dozier wrote a telling article in the *Greenville News* about the state of downtown and Police Chief Harold Jennings's plan to "clean up" the area. Jennings vowed, "No prostitutes. No flocks of boisterous teenagers driving the streets. No beggars. No winos. When it's all over, an 80-year-old lady can step out of the Poinsett Hotel and walk to a gift shop without seeing people begging and panhandling. West of Main the alleys and deserted warehouses are infested with drunks, prostitutes, hoodlums, and drug pushers. Derelicts sleep in a hole in the ground in one West Washington Street alley." The west-of-Main area Dozier referred to included Sanitary's block. The long-standing business succumbed to the circumstances of the era and closed in 1977.

7

Woolworth's Lunch Counter

Owner: F.W. Woolworth's Department Store
Years open: 1936–94
Location: 7 North Main Street

One of the most iconic department stores in United States history is Woolworth's. It's first Greenville location opened in 1910 in the Cleveland building on South Main Street. By 1936, the company's popularity had skyrocketed, and it opened a huge new store at the corner of North Main and West Washington Streets. One of the big advances of the facility was that it was fully air conditioned. According to the *Greenville News* account, this new location featured a lunch counter "at which all types of soft drinks and lunches will be served. As an added attraction for opening day, the department will serve a turkey dinner for $0.25." This lunch counter, however, was for whites only.

Woolworth's menu was typical of lunch counters at the time, including such staple sandwiches as bacon and tomato, baked cheese and ham, chicken salad, ham and egg salad and grilled cheese. At the soda fountain, guests could choose from items like a deluxe tulip sundae (ice cream covered in crushed fruit or fresh fruits in season) for $0.25, a super jumbo banana split for $0.39, an extra-rich ice cream soda for $0.25 or a malted shake for $0.25. Going to Woolworth's to enjoy a $0.25 banana split on a Saturday afternoon would be a highlight for many kids throughout the years.

This 1895 photo shows the Cleveland building at the corner of South Main and E. McBee Streets. In 1910, it became the first location for Woolworth's in Greenville. *Courtesy of the South Carolina Room, Greenville County Library System.*

Woolworth's lunches were an integral part of many Greenvillians' daily lives and were a convenient food service. What ultimately made the restaurant important in our city's history is the role it played during the crucial time of the civil rights movement of the 1960s. Back in 1953, when the Main Street store wanted to extend its building onto West Washington and into the Wallace Building, it also sought to add dining space with a new lunch counter for blacks. However, segregation laws prohibited restaurants from serving both races in the same room. According to the *Greenville News* report, Woolworth's attorney successfully appealed the city council to amend the law by arguing that all downtown stores might be violating that provision. Consequently, the council approved the request and amended the law that "will permit Negros and White persons in the same room if separate facilities (dishes are to be of different color or design) are used and the facilities for the two races are separated by at least 35 feet." While this added an eating option for blacks in the heart of downtown, it was certainly not equal justice in its execution. Much more needed to be done.

The sit-in movement to push for integration of blacks and whites at public establishments began in February 1960 in Greensboro, North Carolina, at the lunch counter of a Woolworth's Department Store. Black students in many other southern cities took the cue from their Greensboro pioneering

Above: The Woolworth's building at the corner of South Main and West Washington Streets was built in 1953 and closed in 1994. It was the site of civil rights sit-in demonstrations in the early 1960s. *Courtesy of the Camperdown Mill Historical Society.*

Left: Students from Sterling High School and others from the local African American community held sit-in demonstrations at the Woolworth's lunch counter. *Courtesy of the Greenville Historical Society, Joe Jordan Collection.*

predecessors, and it soon became a movement of epic proportions. Following demonstrations in Rock Hill and Columbia, South Carolina, the movement came to Greenville and involved students from Sterling High School.

Following sit-ins at Greenville's public library, the first restaurant sit-ins took place on July 18, 1960, at two downtown lunch counters, W.T. Grant Co. and S.H. Kress & Co. The demonstration was organized by Charles Helms, a white minister from Atlanta who went to Greenville to work with black church congregations. While Mr. Helms was permitted to eat at the whites-only counter, the eight local black students who were with him were not. According to news reports, the lunch counter was closed and roped off after the demonstration but was opened again after the black protesters left.

The Sterling Square statue at the corner of South Main and West Washington Streets was sculpted by Mariah Kirby-Smith to commemorate the civil rights movement that took place on that corner at Woolworth's Department Store. *From author's collection.*

The next week, a 9:00 p.m. curfew was enforced to "ease the racial unrest." A second sit-in event took place on August 2, involving twenty to thirty blacks at W.T. Grant Co., S.H. Kress & Co., H.L. Green Co. and F.W. Woolworth Co.—all of which closed their lunch counters to clear the areas. No arrests were made at these sit-ins. The next day, demonstrators returned to those stores while others attempted to play a game of softball in the white-only Cleveland Park. On August 24, the first picketing demonstration was held and included the sidewalk in front of F.W. Woolworth's. Those involved carried signs reading, "Behold, I stand at the Door and They Won't Let Me Eat," "Stop Segregation" and "Give Respectable Eating Equality Now."

In September, Woolworth's and other department stores formally agreed to end segregation at their lunch counters nationally, but "local customs" continued. In May 1963, *Peterson vs. the City of Greenville* went to the Supreme Court and decided that segregation at eating establishments was unconstitutional. Subsequently, Greenville wiped all such ordinances from its laws. In the words of local black lawyer Willie Smith, who helped push the case through, it was "a landmark case." Successfully integrating at eating establishments is what led to other businesses, such as movie theaters and hotels, doing the same.

One of the Sterling High School protesters at the library was Jesse Jackson. His participation in the civil rights movement in Greenville led to a lifelong commitment to involvement and leadership for equal rights. His national status was highlighted by his candidacy for the president of the United States in 1984 and 1988.

The Woolworth's Main Street location closed in 1994. It was a loss for many low- and fixed-income families who could enjoy shopping and experiencing downtown at a more affordable price than the new boutique shops and European-style cafés that were coming into place at that time.

The legacy of Greenville's momentous civil rights movement lives on with a life-size bronze statue by Mariah Kirby Smith on the corner of West Washington and South Main Streets, where the Woolworth's store stood for eighty-three years. This corner was also where each year at the Christmas parade, the Sterling High School band would "show out" to the many alumni and friends who would line the street. The statue shows two Sterling High School students walking proudly and confidently down a set of stairs.

PART II

1945–70: DINERS, DRIVE-INS AND DESTINATIONS

THE DOWNTURN OF GREENVILLE'S RESTAURANT GROWTH DURING the Great War turned around quickly in the succeeding decades. Downtown flourished during the late 1940s and into the '50s, with many new restaurants patronized by a steady stream of shoppers from department stores like Ivey's, Woolworth's, Belk's, Meyers-Arnold and Grant's. The meat-and-three restaurants and lunch counters were always popular options. As suburbs developed outside of the downtown core, restaurants spread to all parts of town and the mill villages.

A variety of ethnic foods appeared for the first time in this era, including Italian dishes at Capri's and Perone's, Chinese food at the New China Restaurant, European entrées at the Dutch Mill and Mexican fare at El Matador. Members of the Greek community continued to run a large percent of Greenville restaurants, many with American fare, like the Rainbow Drive-In, and others with authentic dishes, like the Greek Restaurant (Never on Sunday).

A new dynamic emerged with the carhop, drive-in culture, which was followed by the arrival of fast-food restaurants like the first McDonalds on Pleasantburg Drive. Formal dining options grew by the late 1960s, with steak houses offering live bands and entertainers.

1

Capri's No. 2

Owners: Julius and Helen Capri and Guido and Audrey Capri
Years open: 1945–95
Location: 1605 Augusta Street and 3505 Augusta Street

Pizza can be found in restaurants and homes all around Greenville now, but it first became available to Greenville patrons through Julius Nino "Cap" Capri. He was born in L'Aquila, Italy, but immigrated to Gallitzin, Pennsylvania (near Altoona), where his in-laws, Harry and Livia Sullivan, and his parents, Guido and Emma, lived. Julius and his wife, Helen, came to Greenville, South Carolina, during World War II to work at the newly created Greenville Army Air Base.

Julius had an important job as the foreman of all civilian mechanics working at the base. Many of the soldiers stationed there, like Capri, came down from northern states where ethnic foods were more commonplace. Comforting Italian dishes like pizza, ravioli and spaghetti were readily found in northern homes, but the airmen craved them in Greenville, and authentic dishes were nowhere to be found. Greenville native and historian Tom Brissey remembers that his father, an assistant foreman under Capri, would get to taste pizza when Julius brought it to the base in his lunchbox and shared it with him. Sometimes Brissey would bring it home for his other family members to try.

A portrait of Julius and Helen Capri, founders of the Capri family of restaurants. *Courtesy of the Capri family.*

The family's traditional story is that Helen Capri began making homemade Italian dishes once a week to satisfy the soldiers' requests. By the time the war ended and the air base was winding down, the Capris were ready to trade in their home-kitchen business for a commercial one. The first location was at 1605 Augusta Street and became the first restaurant to serve pizza in Greenville. The building they bought was a long, wood cabin structure, which previously held Mrs. Bill's Bar-B-Q. Prior to Mrs. Bill's, Shoeless Joe Jackson had a barbecue restaurant there for a couple years when returning to Greenville after being banished from professional baseball.

When Capri's opened in 1945, it proudly announced that Greenvillians could now have "real Italian spaghetti" offered on a daily basis. Not only could guests enjoy spaghetti and pizza, but they could also choose from steak and seafood accompanied by a nice selection of wine and beer. Within a few years, it was advertising fifty-cent lunches, including French fries, dessert and coffee or milk included with pizza. Ravioli was another dish that was pioneered for the first time in Greenville.

Lunch began at noon, and service lasted until 11:00 p.m. In 1948, it moved to 1609 Augusta Road (next door to the original location) to expand capacity and service options. Not only was breakfast added, starting at 6:30 a.m., but dinner service was also extended to 1:00 a.m. Curb service was added in 1949, and this was one of the first Greenville restaurants to offer the convenience. Two years later, the address changed to 1611 Augusta Road, with the addition of a full-fledged drive-in service. The bonus attraction was that not only could guests inside the restaurant enjoy watching television, but there was also a television installed outside for drive-in customers. Meanwhile, Julius Capri's sister Susie and her husband, Ed Berardinelli, moved to Greenville to help out with the family business.

The 1950s was a decade of significant expansion for Capri's. Opportunity knocked in 1953, when the Plantation House farther down the street at

3505 Augusta closed after just eight months in business. The paint was practically still wet at the new building when the family moved Capri's down the street. Within weeks, Capri's was open for business with a grand opening on November 1. The old Greenville Army Air Base that had brought Julius Capri to Greenville was now called Donaldson Air Force Base. Twenty-two hundred men were stationed there, and it was called the "airlift capital of the world." The new Capri's was much closer to the busy air base. It was adjacent to the busy Interstate 85 and only minutes away from the Greenville Country Club.

When Capri's moved out of its 1611 Augusta Road address, Pete's took over the space, making it the establishment's third drive-in location. At the same time, the Capri family opened a new restaurant in the heart of downtown at 111 West Washington Street. Ed and Susie Berardinelli were the proprietors. With multiple locations, the downtown Capri's was called Capri's No. 1 while the 3505 Augusta Road location was called Capri's No. 2.

The new building for Capri's No. 2 was a much larger facility and included second floor living space for Julius and Helen's family and a private dining space for parties. Though curb service was no longer part of the operation, hours were extended to serve guests until 3:00 a.m. Capri's No. 3 opened at 15 Augusta Road in 1957, next door to the popular Greenville Bowling

Ed and Susie Berardinelli in front of Capri's No. 1 on Washington Street. *Courtesy of Tina Berardinelli Collins.*

This November 1, 1952 advertisement invites guests to dine at Capri's new location at 3505 Augusta Road. *Courtesy of the* Greenville News, USA TODAY NETWORK.

Center. Meanwhile, Capri's No. 2 began mass producing its Italian dishes to offer take-home, heat-and-serve frozen meals, including pizza pies with meat sauce, baked lasagna, ravioli and chicken cacciatore. In January 1959, further expansion brought Capri's No. 4 to 500 East Stone Avenue, next to Sears, Roebuck & Co. Department Store and the rapidly expanding suburbs along the superhighway.

The original Capri's on Augusta continued to do good business and began to appeal more and more to families, advertising that the restaurant "especially cater[s] to children's plates." The Sunday family dinners started at just $0.65 for the spaghetti with meat sauce and meat balls. Favorite American Sunday dishes included a fried chicken meal with two vegetables, dessert and a drink for only $0.75; a turkey dinner with all trimmings for $1.00; and a grilled beef tenderloin or country-fried steak dinner for $1.00. Guests celebrating special occasions could splurge on the eight-ounce rock lobster tail for $1.50.

In keeping with the concentration on the Augusta Road, Capri's Pizzeria opened at 401 Augusta Street in 1965, selling pick-up or dine-in pizzas until midnight every night, with Henry Wilburn as proprietor. Being near Greenville High School and the heart of Greenville's West End made it a good choice for regular customers, especially those who wanted to take advantage of the delivery service.

By 1967, Guido and Audrey Capri owned and operated it and had renovated the interior. Franchises for Capri's appeared throughout the area beginning in the 1970s, and several continue to operate in 2020. The original Capri's (No. 2) continued to operate until the 1990s as one of the most beloved restaurants in Greenville history.

2
Gene's Restaurant

Owners: Ted, Bertie, Gene and Ty Eckford
Years open: 1955–2011
Location: 527 Buncombe Street

Gene Eckford, namesake for Gene's Restaurant, grew up on a farm just west of Westminster, South Carolina. After weathering the Depression years as best they could in the country, his family moved to the "big city" of Greenville in 1937. Though Greenville felt the effects of those tough economic times, it was still impressive for young Gene to see all the big buildings, like the Poinsett Hotel and the Woodside Building (the tallest in the state at that time). His father, Ted, also known as "Elmo," got into the restaurant business to make money for his family (similar to Noah Lowe's situation with Fall Street Café earlier that decade in the Camperdown Mill village). He first took over an existing café in the Poinsett Mill village near the Reedy River in downtown Greenville and renamed it Ted's Café. Ted, his wife, Bertie, and Gene, all worked together in the restaurant. Two years later, they moved the café to 859 Buncombe Street, next to the busy Ideal Laundry. By 1943, Ted had moved the business down the street a little farther toward Main Street to 531 Buncombe Street, still keeping the name Ted's Café.

According to an interview with the *Greenville News*, Gene spent the next few years away of his family's business, working at the Monaghan Mill and later for J.P. Stevens. He realized how much he missed the restaurant business and came

WOW!
What a Meal!

Gene's Special All Week

BARBECUED

BEEF STEAK

Choice of 3
Vegetables
Beverage
Dessert

85¢

Gene's
restaurant

Opp. Coca Cola Plant
531 Buncombe

A 1959 advertisement for one of Gene's meat-and-three specials. *Courtesy of the* Greenville News, USA TODAY NETWORK.

back to run the restaurant in 1955, when his father's health began to decline. That is when the business that his dad had built up for him was renamed Gene's Restaurant, and a true landmark for downtown Greenville was born. The current location at 527 Buncombe Street was built in 1958 next to the previous location.

For Greenville, Gene's was the quintessential meat-and-three restaurant. According to John T. Edge, director of the Southern Foodways Alliance, in a 2016 interview for Eater, "As the Southern worker transitioned from farm to city, you see this meal arise. To me, a meat and three is the example of country to city transition, farm to urban transition. It was food for people who plowed the back forty [acres], reinterpreted for people who work at desks and in factories, catching lunch breaks in the city instead of returning home for lunch."

Gene's story fits perfectly with Edge's description of the meal's evolution. The meat-and-three offered a lot of food, but its environment was more like the dining room table at home. By contrast, cafeterias offered a lot of food, but their facilities were generally very large and meant to feed a lot of people in a quick manner.

Classic features of a meat-and-three restaurant menu include:

- A list of proteins to choose—one as the main entrée for the dish, often including meatloaf, fried chicken, hamburger steak with gravy, fried catfish, pot roast and pork tenderloin
- A list of fresh sides, from which the guest chooses three, including green beans, fried okra, collards, mac 'n' cheese, creamed corn, coleslaw, fried green tomatoes and mashed potatoes
- Cornbread, biscuit or roll
- A drink (often sweet tea)
- Dessert

The comforts of a home-cooked meal, familiar faces, southern hospitality and a place for friends, neighbors, and coworkers to sit around a table and talk is what Gene's was all about. Even beyond the familiar faces, it would not be unusual for a new customer to come in and feel at home. If the "stranger" kept coming back, the hospitality Gene and the longtime workers offered would convince him or her to be a regular. Gene would greet visitors as they came in, come around to their tables to see how everything was going and see each guest out at the cash register and invite them back. He was the type of person who would make anyone feel welcome and no matter their status, dress or station in life would make them feel like they were the most important customer. When Gene's daughter, Andri, was a little girl, she would sit on the counter and help by offering toothpicks to customers on their way out. The *Greenville News* reported that a customer named J.T. Cox wrote to the restaurant and said, "I want to tell you about the prettiest picture in town. It's that little child at Gene's Restaurant. She's the daughter of Gene Eckford, the owner, and she's the cutest thing you've ever seen. She sits up there on the showcase and passes out toothpicks and invites people to come back. It's just the sweetest thing you've ever seen."

That is the kind of hospitality that kept people coming back. It was the "regular" crowd that loved and supported Gene's for so long. It wasn't a tourists' spot. When Gene's opened, downtown was still thriving, and people came from all around the area to visit. By the late 1960s and early '70s, fewer people came downtown. The destinations were gone. However, the regulars still came to Gene's. Meat-and-threes like his brought together people from all walks of life.

Along with Tommy's Ham House, Gene's was a must-stop for politicians coming through town to garner grassroots support. Strom Thurmond, Ernest Hollings, David Beasley and Jack Kemp are a few who stopped in while campaigning. Whether you were a politician, attorney, downtown office worker, judge, banker, police officer or secretary, mealtime at Gene's was a true cross section of Greenville's community.

Jim Wilson was one of the familiar faces. He worked at Piedmont Printmakers and always ate at the counter, stopping in for breakfast nearly every weekday morning to meet up with his friends. Jim recalls that the longtime cook, Mary Henderson, would gladly make dishes for them that weren't on the menu, like brains and eggs or an old-school military meal like an S.O.S. (sh—— on a shingle, a.k.a. chipped beef and gravy on toast). Michael Stone went to eat there with many coworkers from Fluor Daniel's headquarters on Main Street. Marion Uldrick took his family there in the '60s and '70s, and when his daughter Lisa grew up and worked at BB&T bank, he met her at least once a week to have lunch at Gene's. Lisa continued the tradition with her kids. Jill Garrett grew up on Butler Avenue (which bordered Gene's) and remembers going to Gene's all the time. When the family was finished eating, she always looked forward to the piece of bubble gum Gene would give her.

Into the 1990s and 2000s, when Greenville's downtown was reviving with office workers, residents and things to do, Gene's continued to be family owned and operated, just like when he was young. In gratitude for his community and for many decades of patronage, Gene offered a free Thanksgiving meal to anyone who would come in 1997. That's the kind of guy he was.

When Gene's health declined in 2008, he could manage to go in only a few times a week before he passed away in 2010. His son, Ty Eckford, took over the business but couldn't keep it afloat for very long. Longtime regular Tom Brissey began eating at Gene's weekly in 1959 and was there when the last meat-and-three dinner was served in 2011.

3

Never on Sunday

Owners: Nick and Iris Tassiopoulos; Iris Turner
Years open: 1968–2016
Location: 210 East Court Street

The house at 210 East Court Street has been home to Iris Tassiopoulos nearly all her life. After she moved to Greenville, South Carolina, from Athens, Greece, as a teenager in 1957, Iris started an alteration shop on the second floor of the building. She found a welcoming family in the local Greek community, many of whom were involved in restaurants. Iris made connections of her own with locals who loved her seamstress skills and friendly personality. According to a *Greenville News* interview, Iris took a trip back to Greece to visit family and met Nick Tassiopoulos. Knowing they were meant for one another, the couple married within a month. Shortly after they came to Greenville in 1968, Nick longed to return to his homeland. Iris wanted stay and decided to start a restaurant on the first floor of the building where she had worked for the past decade. Nick didn't have any prior cooking experience, so Iris took a month-long vacation from her upstairs seamstress job and taught her husband how to make all the classic Greek dishes that would be on the menu.

The cozy restaurant had only two small rooms for seating and the kitchen in back. After making necessary renovations, it opened in 1968 with the straightforward name of Greek Restaurant. While many other Greek

Exterior of the home that housed Never on Sunday Greek Restaurant from 1968 until 2016. *From author's collection.*

families in town had restaurants, their menus were primarily filled with popular American dishes like hamburgers, hot dogs, French fries, New York strip steak and meat-and-three selections. The Tassiopouloses, however, concentrated their menu on the dishes that were true to their roots.

For appetizers, guests enjoyed a selection including chicken lemon soup, tiropetes (pastry with cheese, eggs and butter) and spinach pie. The Greek salad was, of course, a customer favorite, and Nick's homemade (secret recipe) dressing made it unique. Main dishes focused little on beef and more on proteins like lamb and chicken, often with highly flavorful rice and vegetable sides. Entrées included lamb stew, chicken pelafee (chicken broiled in sauce and seasoned with Greek spices over a bed of rice), pastichio (macaroni with ground beef and cheese), dolmades (ground beef and rice rolled in grape leaves), keftedes (ground beef and cheese formed into meatballs, fried and served with potatoes), moussaka (ground beef with eggplant and cheese), shish kebab, souvlaki, gyros and stewed beef with potatoes. Desserts like galaktoboureko (an egg custard) and baklava (a flaky pastry with pecans, almonds, butter and honey) were the perfect ending to an authentic Greek three- or four-course meal. For the guest who wanted a non-Greek option, a hamburger steak and fries or a pasta and meatball dish were available.

Service was offered for lunch and dinner Monday through Saturday but never on Sunday. It wasn't until 1977 that Nick and Iris's Greek Restaurant changed its name to Never on Sunday. The story goes that a customer called to ask if they were open on Sunday and Iris replied, "Never on Sunday." She told her husband to have a new sign made, and the name was adopted. Needless to say, no one ever asked about Sunday hours again.

Over the years, friends from the local Greek community loved to have a taste of home at Never on Sunday. Many regulars, though, were native southerners or locals who had transplanted from other parts of the United States. The restaurant didn't change over the decades—the menu, pots, dishes and décor remained largely the same over the fifty-plus years it was open. One of the few things that changed was the addition of photos of friends, regular customers and their families on one of the restaurant walls. People who came to enjoy the food in the '60s and '70s brought their kids and grandkids back to enjoy Iris and Nick's food in the following decades.

According to a *Greenville News* interview, while Iris and Nick were basically the sole employees for the entire history of the restaurant, they occasionally had their niece Iris help with waitressing on the weekends. Nick injured his knee in 2014, and she filled in as cook with her aunt as guide. Nick and Iris asked if she would like to take over the restaurant and she agreed. Iris Turner continued the family tradition for several years, but the restaurant closed in 2016. The legacy of a husband-wife team cooking authentic ethnic food in that space continued in fall of that same year, when Chef Nelo Mayar and her husband opened Aryana Restaurant serving Afghan cuisine.

Never on Sunday Pastichio

1 medium onion, chopped
2 tablespoons olive oil
1 pound ground beef
salt and pepper to taste
oregano to taste
garlic to taste
1 tablespoon tomato paste

1 pound macaroni
1 cup shredded Myzithra cheese
10 eggs
16 ounces milk

In a large saucepan, brown the onions in olive oil. Add the ground beef to the onions and let cook on medium heat for thirty minutes. Add salt, pepper, oregano, garlic and tomato paste to the meat and cook for thirty more minutes. Boil the macaroni and then drain well. In a large bowl, mix the cooked macaroni with the Myzithra cheese. In a casserole dish, spread one layer of macaroni and cheese along the bottom. Add a layer of meat mixture and then another layer of macaroni and cheese. Blend the eggs in a separate bowl and bring the milk to a boil. When the milk boils, add the eggs. Put the egg and milk mixture on the top layer of the casserole. Bake at 350 degrees for one hour. Be careful to not allow the top layer to burn.

4

The Rainbow Drive-In

Owners: Pete Kythas, Gus Kythas, Jimmy Hryikos and Leon and Patti Kolokithas
Years open: 1959–2009
Location: 1218 New Buncombe Road (Poinsett Highway)

The Rainbow Drive-In originated on January 7, 1959, with a local Greek man named C.N. Alexander. He grew up in the same part of Evrytania, Greece, as his friend Pete Kythas, who, along with his cousin Jimmy Hrysikos, soon took over the drive-in. None of them could speak English, but they knew how to work hard, how to cook and how to be friendly.

When the Rainbow opened, Greenville was in the midst of the drive-in restaurant craze that began in 1921 at Kirby's Pig Stand in Dallas, Texas. Campbell's Pharmacy on Augusta Road was the first restaurant to feature the service in Greenville. By the early 1940s, curb service began to show up in Greenville to cater to the freedom afforded by automobiles. Stanley's Drive-In Liquor Shop offered convenient booze. Greenville Laundry and Cleaners and Ideal Laundry offered curb service. The Skyland Drive-In Theater came to New Buncombe Road in 1948. Restaurants offering curb service began go show up in the early 1940s, too, like Nick's Best Diner on Main Street and the Pickwick on Augusta Road. Out of the drive-in culture emerged one of America's favorite pastimes—cruising. Cruising Greenville in the 1930s and '40s was less about going to restaurant parking lots and more about cruising Main Street. In these early decades, the typical time for cruising Main was in

An early 1960s view of the original Rainbow Drive-In exterior. *Courtesy of Leon Kolokithas.*

the late afternoons after school. Cars would pass one another, and teenagers would throw notes from car window to car window. If you were lucky, you could get a response to your note by the time you passed the car again the next time around. After multiple passes up and down the street, kids might head over to Campbell's Pharmacy on Augusta Road.

With the onset of World War II, all aspects of society were affected, including gas rationing. Cruising and restaurant curb service stopped during the war years, and automobile food trays started appearing in basement sale advertisements in the *Greenville News*. When the war ended, curb service resumed, and Greenville's first restaurant that billed itself as a drive-in, Cully's Drive-In, opened in 1946 at 101 Cleveland Street. By the time the Rainbow Drive-In opened thirteen years later on New Buncombe Road, there were twenty-six other drive-in restaurants in town.

A few months after opening the Rainbow, Pete Kythas's brother Gus moved from Augusta, Georgia, to Greenville to help run the restaurant. Gus's wife, Maria, and their son, Leon, stayed in Augusta while Gus got acclimated to Greenville and financially stable enough to bring his family. When Maria and Leon finally arrived in May 1961, they moved into the small wooden house that Pete, Jimmy and Gus were living in at the back of the restaurant's property. Leon was only five when he started helping out. He went to Arrington Elementary school and was the first in the family to formally learn to speak English. The rest of the family learned the language from him, radio, television and working at the restaurant.

In the early years, the building had the kitchen and one long counter for service inside while the carhops attended to orders from cars pulling under

Left: A family enjoys a meal at the single original counter during the Rainbow Drive-In's early days. *Courtesy of Leon Kolokithas.*

Right: Drive-ins like the Rainbow afforded the convenience of carhops bringing the food to customer's cars. *Courtesy of Leon Kolokithas.*

the awning outside. Tables were added later for additional seating inside the restaurant. Carhops were kept busy bringing orders to cars in the parking lot. Favorite menu items included the sliced BBQ beef, roast pork, minced BBQ, fried chicken, BLT and steak sandwich. However, hands down, the iconic meal that most patrons kept coming back for was the chili cheeseburger, onion rings and homemade slaw. The kids who spent all their money on gas might order a pine float, a glass of water with a toothpick. Teenagers from the surrounding high schools, especially Parker High School, flocked to the Rainbow as part of their cruising or hanging out rituals on Friday nights after the football games and on Saturday nights.

If you were lucky, you could score a parking spot for a while in one of the drive-ins to meet and talk to other kids. According to some people, "the 'good girls' stayed in the car, and the 'bad girls' got out and roamed around." For kids with nothing else to do, cruising the drive-ins and Main Street was *the* thing to do at night—all in generally good, clean fun. Guys would spend all day polishing their souped-up cars to show off at night. Girls would primp and pick which outfits and accessories were the best to wear.

Wade Hampton High School students typically went to the Clock Drive-In on Wade Hampton Boulevard, continuing to Main Street in downtown, then to the Poinsett Drive-In and, finally, back to Main Street. However, any combination of the Carolina Drive-In on Buncombe, the Clock on Stone or

Wade Hampton, the Palmetto Drive-In on Laurens, Li'l Rebel Drive-In on Pleasantburg and one of Pete's Drive-In locations was common.

While at the Palmetto, a Pink Lady drink was the usual choice for the girls. A Greek man nicknamed Sho-Sho at Pete's on Pendleton could easily stack a row of ten hot dogs on his arm to assemble and entertain. Carhops at Li'l Rebel Drive-In had a choreographed dance step to the sounds coming from the jukebox that was piped to the outdoor speakers. Windows or convertible tops were down, the radio was playing music (usually from WQOK) and the teenagers were constantly on the lookout for who was in the cars passing them. At most stoplights, a carload of kids would get out to do a Chinese fire drill. When on Main Street, the boundaries for the cruising route were circling around the Daniel Building or Downtowner Motor Inn on North Main and slowly dragging down to South Main, turning right on Court Street next to the Poinsett Hotel to circle around and go back to North Main. After cruising Main Street, drivers might either park for a while and sit on their hoods to talk to others or head on for another trip to a favorite drive-in like the Rainbow. People like Angie Sprouse, Linda Barton, Marie Poole Carter and Brenda Nix were among the many who had their first dates with their future husbands there. Judy Browning Turner's boyfriend asked her to marry him while at the Rainbow.

When the Rainbow Drive-In opened in the 1950s, this is what Main Street in downtown Greenville looked like. Court Street bordered the Poinsett Hotel on the left and the Liberty Building on the right. This was the primary turnaround point for teenagers dragging Main Street. *Courtesy of the South Carolina Room, Greenville County Library System.*

Leon Kolokithas continued to work with his family at the restaurant and eventually took over ownership. His grandfather, Leonidas, made the famous onion rings and did a lot of the prep work and meat cutting. Uncle Pete continued to cook (especially the chili) and worked front of house before retiring in 1993. Pete's wife, Valentina, and their children also worked at the restaurant. Leon's uncle Jimmy Hryikos also cooked and maintained order in the parking lot before leaving the Rainbow in 1968. Within a few years, he opened the Zorba East Lounge on East Lee Road in Taylors. Leon's father, Gus, worked the register until the time the restaurant closed, while Gus's wife, Maria, helped with the register and waitressing. Leon's daughter Marianthe helped manage the restaurant during her high school years, and his younger daughter, Rosie, became well known as a teenager for her homemade fried apple pies sold in the restaurant. The overall menu remained largely the same throughout the late twentieth century and into the twenty-first century, bringing the faithful regulars back again and again.

In the late 1960s, the Rainbow discontinued the curb service and bricked up the wall facing Poinsett Highway. In the following decade, Greenville's downtown became less populated by restaurants and department stores and more populated by crime, homelessness and prostitution. Cruising the four-lane Main Street, however, continued to be the most popular pastime with the teen and twenties crowd—not only from Greenville but also from surrounding towns and counties. With radios blaring, horns honking and gridlock all night, cruising caused business travelers and residents of downtown to demand solutions from the police. When Mayor Max Heller narrowed Main Street from four lanes to two in 1979, the situation became even worse. Ultimately, police put up barricades at various blocks on Main Street to discourage cruising, but they were often ignored or stolen. New routing to side streets only caused the same problem on those streets. The ongoing struggle between cruisers and police carried on into the 1980s. An ultimate stop to the ritual came with an ordinance against driving by the same spot on Main three times and another against noise.

The era of cruising came to an end in the late '80s. Some drive-in restaurants closed while others like the Rainbow adapted and continued with the patronage of regular dine-in customers. When the Rainbow hosted cruise-in events in its parking lot in the 1990s and 2000s, many nostalgic Greenvillians came with their souped-up old cars to relive memories and talk with old and new friends. The Kolokithas family faithfully served countless locals and visitors in the Greenville community for fifty years before closing on Valentine's Day in 2009.

5

Vince Perone's Restaurant

Owners: Vince Perone, Emil Fritz, Vince Perone Jr. and Steve Perone
Years open: 1956–2002
Location: 1 East Antrim Drive

Vince Perone was born in Hackensack, New Jersey, and first got interested in the food industry after working at a butcher shop in his hometown. He excelled in high school football, and a sports scholarship at Furman University brought him to Greenville, South Carolina, in 1949. After graduating, Perone saw a need for the kind of hearty Italian sandwiches he grew up with in New Jersey. Like Eugenia Duke had done half a century earlier, Perone began production of sandwiches in his home to sell in the community. Since deli meats, which were popular in New England, weren't used much in the South yet, Perone catered to local taste and used spiced ham, bologna, American and white cheese, mayonnaise, mustard and sweet relish. Furman students loved the taste and could afford them at twenty-five cents each.

Vince's friend Emil Fritz helped deliver the popular po' boys and other deli sandwiches. While the dorms were the initial outlet, Perone soon expanded sales through the campus dining hall. Like Mrs. Duke before him, local drugstores like Carpenter Bros. began selling Perone's beefy sandwiches, and the need grew for a storefront operation. In 1958, Perone partnered with Fritz and leased a building near Laurens Road and

The original sandwich board that hung in Vince Perone's Deli at Laurens Road and South Pleasantburg Drive. *Courtesy of Emil Fritz.*

South Pleasantburg. They opened Vince Perone's Deli with carry-out-only service. It was the first deli in Greenville and introduced such items as manicotti, corned beef, lasagna and pastrami. Bread was shipped in from Miami, Florida, and was just the right pairing for the meat. The storefront was a fortuitous move because the newly named Pleasantburg Drive brought access to a rapidly developing area, especially the thirty-five-acre adjacent lot that the McAlister family sold for development. The Pleasantburg Shopping Center across the street was also developing with Woolworth's second Greenville location as an anchor.

Demand for Perone's sandwiches grew, and businessmen would come to find no space to sit. There were stacks of pickle barrels in the kitchen, so people started using them for seating. Vince's mother, Jeannie (known by all as Mama Perone), cooked many of the family's Italian recipes in the kitchen. Demand for her homemade lasagna, cheesecakes and other dishes grew, so the need for a larger restaurant space was met in 1961 at the corner of East Antrim and South Pleasantburg. One of the first customers at the kosher deli was Max Heller, a highly successful Jewish businessman (and later mayor), whose Maxon Shirt Company was down the street. As a reflection of Perone's love and trust for his community, customer's bills were handled on an honor system from the time they

Exterior of the Vince Perone's Delicatessen & Restaurant that opened in 1961 at the corner of East Antrim and South Pleasantburg Drives. *Courtesy of the Perone family.*

opened their first store in 1958 until 1967, when progress demanded a more stringent system. Bills were not handed out when people ordered during that period. After guests would serve themselves at the cafeteria-style counter, they would go to the cash register and tell what they had. They were charged accordingly.

In the early 1970s, the restaurant was enlarged to create a formal dining room called the Forum with enough seating for 450 guests. Perone's authentic Italian flavors were a hit, and the Lasagna alla Mama Perone was the star attraction. This restaurant also brought such gourmet choices as rack of lamb and live Maine lobster to Greenville's culinary scene. The dining room was equipped with a bandstand stage for nightly entertainment and attracted the Tommy Dorsey Band, Count Basie's orchestra, Frank Sinatra Jr., Al Hurt and Glen Miller's Band. Danny Marshall was the Monday through Saturday nightly performer along with female vocalist Charlene Foster.

In 1968, the $10 million McAlister Square opened across the street from Perone's as South Carolina's first fully enclosed mall. The restaurant's ideal location guaranteed decades of continued success as the mall marked the beginning of the emptying of downtown Greenville's department stores and crowds. The suburbs were the future, and Perone's enjoyed patronage from thousands of guests in newly built nearby subdivisions. Soon, locations were added, with a city club and a deli in Asheville and Spartanburg and on Greenville's Main Street in the basement of the Daniel Building and on the second floor of the Meyers-Arnold department store.

In 1972, Perone expanded the Antrim location to seat six hundred guests between the Forum dining room, VIP Club and deli. Beni Mason was a regular stage performer at this time, providing comedy, songs and impressions while guests dined on their favorite Italian dishes, prime rib, shrimp scampi,

A menu from Vince Perone's Forum picturing various performers who entertained guests. *Courtesy of the Perone family.*

crab cakes and more. A buffet selection of Mama's hot Italian dishes and fresh salads catered to the crowds looking for a quick and delicious lunch option. Perone scored a coup in 1979 when he lured the legendary trumpeter Charlie Spivak out of retirement to be a regular entertainer.

Though Vince Perone Jr. and Steve Perone grew up in their father's restaurants, they officially joined the family business in 1976. After three years at the Antrim location, Steve spent the following years expanding the business with three other Perone restaurant locations, and in 1979, he opened the Centre Court Café and the Courtyard Café.

During Ronald Reagan's presidential campaign in 1980, he scheduled a stop at Perone's to have Mama's famous rum cake dessert to celebrate his sixty-ninth birthday. Naturally, the restaurant was filled to capacity. Steve Perone recalls that when Reagan leaned over to blow out the birthday candles on the cake, whipped cream got all over his shirt and pants. The Secret Service was quick to wipe off his shirt and supply him with a new suit jacket, but his pants were not able to be changed. When Reagan went to give his speech, he reached into his pocket to find his notes, but they were still in the other jacket. Not missing a beat, Reagan said, "I can certainly give a speech without my notes, but I'll be damned if I'm going to take my pants off!" The crowd roared with laughter.

George Bush and Jack Kemp also visited Perone's on presidential campaigns, stumping for votes and tasting some of Mama's famous dishes. Another high-profile connection is that whenever Paul Newman and Joanne Woodward came to town (she lived here during high school), they would be sure to get a lemon meringue pie from Perone's.

As Greenville changed in the 1980s, Perone's decided to close the long-standing Forum dining room and VIP Club and convert it to a membership-only, exclusive, ten-thousand-square-foot space called the Greenville City Club. Emile Pandolfi was the nightly entertainer playing classical piano. His six years playing at the City Club launched a career that would take him around the world selling millions of records.

The public could still enjoy familiar lunch and dinner favorites in what was the Lighterside Restaurant, now renamed Vince Perone's Restaurant. The $750,000 renovation seemed to be the right move, as the high-society crowd loved the private club concept, and more than fifteen hundred people signed up in the first year. These big changes in 1985 also included bringing Perone family members into key roles. Vince Perone Jr. moved from managing the Forum and VIP Club to general house manager, while Steve Perone was brought on as general operations

Steve Perone honored his father's legacy and continues to provide the family's recipes for local and national communities through a variety of products in the Perone's Italian Kitchen line. *Courtesy of Steve Perone.*

manager after owning and managing the Centre Court Café in Haywood Mall and the Courtyard Café in Spartanburg. Steve Perone hired a young talent, Tyler Florence, to work at Perone's before he headed off to Johnson & Wales.

In 1993, the Sideline Deli and Bar was added to appeal to the younger crowd and had sports pictures covering the walls. It was a true forerunner of the sports bars of today. Vince Perone was looking to retire from a lifelong dedication to day-to-day operations of restaurant ownership, and he sold his interests in 1996.

Soon, however, Perone's name would be in stores all over the greater Greenville area when he partnered with the Bi-Lo grocery chain. Vince's deli, pizza and rotisserie products in all of their store delis now came with his endorsement under the title of "Vince's." In the advertisements, Vince was quoted as saying, "Come taste the difference in my salads… all are made with natural and delicious ingredients. After just one bite you'll love them."

While the restaurants that the Perone family built up were all closed by 2002, Steve Perone resurrected the core family recipes by starting the Perone's Italian Kitchen line of pasta products in 2014. The business initially sold out of a local farmer's market but has since grown to multiple grocery chains and local specialty shops. The homemade marinara sauces, lasagnas, Italian seasoning spice blend, extra virgin olive oil with herbs and almond biscotti bites continue the family legacy that has supplied great food and memories for more than sixty years.

6
Ye Olde Fireplace

Owners: Charlie Grubbs and Cecil Bagwell; Steve Smalls
Years open: 1960–90
Location: 1896 South Pleasantburg Drive

Charlie Grubbs and Cecil Bagwell opened Ye Olde Fireplace on Pleasantburg Boulevard in 1960. Its only competition for steaks outside of downtown was the new Open Hearth Steak House on Wade Hampton Boulevard, but for steaks and dancing, it was the Charcoal Steak House on Augusta Road. Grubbs and Bagwell, however, combined twenty years of restaurant experience and ambition to create the "showplace of the South." The new building, of course, featured a large and inviting fireplace. The spacious dining room could seat one hundred guests, and the menu centered on aged charbroiled steaks.

Within months, the restaurant became a regular meeting place for many local groups, like the newly formed Pleasantburg Rotary Club and the Augusta Road Kiwanis Club. The more casual family dining room served the everyday lunch and dinner crowds, while five additional private dining rooms were added in 1962, including Ye Olde Pub, the Windsor Room and the King Charles Room.

In 1963, the combination of fine steak dining and dancing came to downtown Greenville with the expansion of Ye Olde Fireplace into Hotel Greenville's former dining rooms. It had a capacity of five hundred guests.

The Pleasantburg location's original partner Cecil Bagwell took ownership of the hotel's restaurant. A year later, Bagwell left Ye Olde Fireplace and added competition with the opening of his new entertainment dining restaurant spot the Rib and Loin Steak House just up the road on Pleasantburg.

For entertainment, guests in the early '60s enjoyed such performers as the Harry Fraser Orchestra and the lilting voice of Gomer Pyle. By 1966, Grubbs had adopted a policy of hosting bigger name bands. That's when Charlie Spivak, one of the United States' greatest trumpet players from the big band era, first appeared at the restaurant. This was not Spivak's first visit to Greenville, though. In the early 1940s, he performed several times at the Carolina Theater in downtown Greenville, and his band was voted "the sweetest band in the land" in the *Downbeat* magazine's reader's poll. After a twenty-year hiatus, Spivak was ready to stay and put his roots down in Greenville. By then, Spivak had earned the reputation as "the man who plays the sweetest trumpet in the world," and locals could now hear him play six nights a week as the in-house performer in the King Charles Room. He got his start in the late 1920s playing New York City clubs with the Ben Pollack Band but soon became the sideman in the Tommy and Jimmy Dorsey Band. In 1967, Dorsey reunited with Charlie to play at the restaurant as the featured act of the Heart Ball fundraising event.

By the late 1960s, seafood had become an equal player on the menu. Fresh Maine lobsters stuffed with crabmeat and a daily oyster and seafood bar appeared, and the restaurant featured a great deal for family dining room guests with a fried flounder filet with baked potato, salad, bread and a drink for only $1.99. The restaurant's reputation as the "home of the big bands" was established with appearances from the Glenn Miller Orchestra, Woody Herman, Count Basie, Sammy Kaye and the Billy May Band. Some of these same bands, however, also appeared around town at Vince Perone's Forum and at the Rib and Loin Steak House. The world-famous Charlie Spivak performing his theme song "Stardreams" could be found exclusively at Ye Olde Fireplace.

Devastation came to the restaurant, Greenville and the world in 1975, when Spivak's friend and fellow bandmate for twenty-five years, saxophonist Charles Russo, was tragically murdered. Two armed gunman broke in just after closing when staff and band members were still there. One of the nervous gunmen thought Russo was making a wrong move and shot him in the chest. The thieves made off with thousands of dollars and jewelry and were never caught. It's perhaps the most infamous cold case in Greenville history.

Somehow, the band played on, and Spivak ultimately recorded seven albums at Ye Olde Fireplace. The first was *Charlie Spivak at the King Charles Room*, followed by *Night Train, Born Free* and *A Night at Ye Olde Fireplace.*

Charlie Spivak went into semiretirement in 1978, and Herb Howell joined as a weekly entertainer in the Windsor Room. In a 1979 interview with the *Greenville News*, Spivak said that he had grown "bored with inactivity" and began performing Tuesday through Saturday nights at Ye Olde Fireplace's rival down the street, Vince Perone's Forum. Spivak said that Perone made him an offer that he couldn't refuse.

A few years later, Steve Smalls, the owner of rival dance and steak destination the Charcoal Steak House bought out Charlie Grubbs and took over Ye Olde Fireplace. Sea Breeze was the new house band, playing a variety of music (ballroom, swing, beach and country) Monday through Saturday evenings. The big band sound from the likes of Guy Lombardo, Tommy Dorsey, Woody Herman and Buddy Rich continued to be heard there but only at special engagements a few times a year. The menu remained centered on steak and seafood.

As times changed and fans of the big band and older dancing styles began to fade, Smalls converted the former overflow/private dining area into a family-centered seafood restaurant called the Crab Pot. Guests continued to be entertained by the Gene Brown Combo and Stormy Weather until it finally closed in January 1990.

PART III

1970–90: CHANGES IN AND OUT OF DOWNTOWN

THE DOWNTOWN RESTAURANT SCENE THAT WAS THE HEART of Greenville's society since the start of the century began to change in the 1970s. Main Street was the center of shopping for the city's entire history until suburban malls started to come in the late 1960s. McAlister Square on Pleasantburg Drive came first in 1968, followed by the Bell Tower Mall on University Drive in 1970. Even though Bell Tower was near downtown, it was not walkable to the core of Main Street, especially with the notorious drugs, crime and prostitution in the West End and Reedy River area. The Greenville Mall on Woodruff Road came in 1978 and was quickly followed by Haywood Mall on Haywood Road in 1980. Without downtown as a shopping destination, restaurants relied on downtown office workers from places like banks, government buildings, the Daniel Building and the *Greenville News*. Some downtown stalwarts like Gene's, Carpenter Bros. Drug Store, Woolworth's Lunch Counter, Never on Sunday and Fall Street Café survived the changes while others like the Sanitary and Boston Lunch did not.

Many chain restaurants opened in the 1970s, taking customers from the independent, local restaurants that were popular for so long. Ryan's Family Steak House started as a local Greenville restaurant on Laurens Road but soon became one of the nation's most successful chains of buffet-style restaurants.

The character of downtown's architecture changed dramatically in the 1960s and early '70s. Older buildings were either painted, covered with "modern" metal façades or torn down. Most of the new buildings were in the simplistic, concrete Brutalist style. The teenagers who continued to enjoy cruising Main Street at night became the largest social crowd occupying the area, much to the dismay of city police and others who considered them a nuisance. Downtown needed a fresh vision for the future, and Austrian-born Mayor Max Heller provided it. Under Heller leadership, Main Street's aesthetic was transformed from an open and concrete look to intimate, green and pedestrian-friendly. In 1979, the four-lane Main Street was narrowed to two, wide sidewalks were added and trees were planted to create a canopy.

In the 1980s, the Hyatt Regency brought business travelers and conventions to North Main, while across the street, condominiums and restaurants appeared. The seeds for an attractive and mixed-use downtown were planted.

The Upstate's growing international business clientele like Bosch and Michelin influenced Greenville's economy and inspired new ethnic restaurants to contribute to the European feel Heller wanted for downtown. Pioneering examples include Red Baron's German cuisine in 1975, Ristorante Bergamo's Italian fare in 1986 and Addy's Dutch and Indonesian flavors in 1989. Other important restaurants opening in the '80s included the vegetarian Annie's Natural Café, the Bijou Bar & Grille, Sophisticated Palate and Maureen's.

Greenville's fine dining scene made significant strides in the 1980s, with the opening of the Fishmarket, Stax's Peppermill and Seven Oaks. Each of them brought formally trained chefs to create levels of flavor new to Greenville patrons. The restaurants also had elegant décor and environments to accompany the haute cuisine.

1

Haus Edelweiss

Owners: Fritz and Margie Emich and Heinrich and Irmgard Looser;
   Ivan Block; Beck Brissey; Fred and Carol Boerin
Years open: 1979–2015
Location: 445 East Stone Avenue; 903 Wade Hampton Boulevard

When Margie Emich and Irmgard Looser opened Haus Edelweiss at 445 East Stone Avenue in 1979, the occasion was celebrated with German food, drinks and live accordion music. Twenty-seven years earlier, Margie had come to the United States (initially to Philadelphia) from Austria, and Irmgard had come from Germany. After years of missing the authentic foods of their homelands, friends began chipping in to buy the German and Austrian ingredients, and Margie and Irmgard made the dishes taught by their families for generations. The Loosers and Emichs also helped to organize annual Oktoberfest celebrations.

Ultimately, they decided to take the experience beyond their gathering of Greenville friends and one-time events and share it with the community on a daily basis. They opened a shop, and _Greenville News_ articles describe how the space was small, primarily acting as a gift shop with small Bavarian home novelties, though it also featured deli meats, salads and other items for patrons to pick up every day except Sunday. Fresh German sausages and other products were brought in from Schaller & Weber in New York and Germany every week. Not only were Margie and Irmgard passionate about bringing authentic Bavarian products and food to Greenville, but they also wore traditional dirndls and explained their cultural wares with their thick accents. The store began to evolve into a place more known and patronized for the food than the household gifts. Many of the regular customers were members of the German-American Club, an organization founded just four years earlier that brought together people in the upstate who were interested in German culture and/or came from places like Germany, Austria and Switzerland. After six years together, Irmgard sold her interest to Margie, who continued to grow and expand the business.

In May 1986, after seven successful years in its Stone Avenue location, Haus Edelweiss moved to the former Steak & Egg restaurant location on Wade Hampton Boulevard. Seating expanded to twenty-two seats, large photos of the Austrian Alps covered the walls and warm wood paneling contributing to a mountain lodge feel. Tucked in a corner was a *Stammtisch*—a type of personal table that can be reserved by a social group. True to its roots, the restaurant also featured a deli and small grocery. A much larger selection of German foods appeared where customers could buy cold cuts or build a custom sandwich from a variety of forty-five meats. Instead of two kinds of liverwurst, they now had eight. The sausage selection grew to nine different types, while tasty favorites like cheeses, smoked meats, goulash, Reuben sandwiches, salmon and herring made it difficult for guests to keep from ordering one of everything. Perhaps the most talked-about and craved item on the menu was Margie's homemade potato salad. Homemade dessert selections rotated daily and could include puff pastries, Frankfurter Kranz, apple cheesecake, apple streusel, apple strudel, Black Forest cherry torte and crumb cake. Early on, Emich thought that the distinct German flavors might be a difficult sell to southerners used to meat-and-threes, grits, fried green tomatoes, fried chicken and collards. However, the concept continued to be widely embraced not only by expat Europeans but also by native Greenvillians.

Margie was the primary cook but was always available to greet both new guests and regular customers. The hospitality she provided and the relationships she formed with patrons helped keep the restaurant busy and thriving. A shocking heart attack forced Margie to sell Haus Edelweiss to Ivan Block in 1990, though Block knew that changing anything would not be good for the business. What Block did was take the great model that was working on Wade Hampton and expanded by opening a larger, second location in the former Waterfall Restaurant space at 301 Haywood Road, near the popular Haywood Mall. It didn't take long for Margie to return to the place she loved, but this time she divided her attention between the Haywood and Wade Hampton locations. The Haywood restaurant could seat up to ninety-nine dinner guests and served Margie's Bavarian favorites from the other store, but it expanded the menu to cater to American tastes, including peached Norwegian salmon, beef Wellington, a mixed grill, steaks, rib-eye, broiled grouper, lobster tail and veal marsala. The extra dining space opened just in time for the coming of BMW's only North American automobile production facility, which opened in 1994. Rapid growth led this facility to become BMW's largest factory in the world. The many new German residents loved to have an authentic taste of Bavaria at Haus Edelweiss.

After nearly fourteen years of managing two restaurants, Margie decided to retire in 2004 and sold the Wade Hampton location to Beck Brissey. Beck had worked part time for Margie for about a year and was a regular customer for longer than that. He had an inside track to buy the restaurant from Margie. Neither knew at the time that Fred and Carol Boerin, who had also been regulars going back to when the Wade Hampton location opened, also wanted to buy it. They were in Europe when they found out Margie was selling, but when they returned, it was too late.

As the new owner, Brissey initially kept the strictly German menu that customers were so familiar with. Over time, however, he added foods from Russia, Italy and other countries. Longtime patrons weren't happy with the changes, and Brissey put it up for sale again in 2007. This time, the Boerins seized the opportunity to bring their favorite restaurant back to life. After a year and a half of preparations and renovations, Haus Edelweiss reopened in 2011 to the celebration of many (though no accordions played this time).

According to Carol, Margie was still in town and agreed to spend more than a year training Carol how to make her authentic dishes. The Boerins bought all her recipes and took the menu back to nearly its original form. Carol and other female workers donned the German dirndls while Fred sported lederhosen. Fred did nearly all the renovations himself. Tragically, Fred passed away of cancer less than a year after opening. Despite her devastation, Carol continued to serve her supportive and grateful customers for several more years. Her daughter, Sara, was a huge help and also learned how to cook many of the dishes. The kitchen manager, Catherine Kilpatrick, was another special help and friend to Carol and her mission to serve the community with a consistency and dedication that began in 1979 when the restaurant opened.

Carol and Fred Boerin in the Haus Edelweiss dining room. *Courtesy of Carol Stewart.*

After four great years of carrying the torch, Carol reluctantly retired from the restaurant business. Patrons will forever be grateful for the extended years of those great Rueben sandwiches and potato salad, sauerbraten and jaeger schnitzel dishes.

For those who love German food and were not able to visit Haus Edelweiss, try this:

Margie's Kraut Recipe

6 strips bacon
1 medium onion
1 can Hengstenberg wine sauerkraut
1 tablespoon brown sugar
⅓ cup applesauce
¼ teaspoon kosher salt
pinch black pepper

Cut bacon in strips and heat until light brown; then remove the bacon pieces from the fat. Chop onions into fine pieces and add to the bacon fat in the heated skillet. Sautee the onions until they're glossy but not brown. Add the sauerkraut, bacon and the rest of the ingredients to the warmed onions and cook for thirty minutes. When finished, add a little water if necessary.

2

Red Baron's

Owner: Marvin and Beth Hambleton
Years open: 1975–98
Location: 118 North Main Street

When Marvin and Beth Hambleton opened their Main Street restaurant in 1975, many restaurants and businesses were shutting down. In the 1970s, downtown restaurants were open during the day for office workers, but they closed early in the evening when the criminals, drunks, prostitutes and cruising crowd were likely to be out. These were the times that the term "little Chicago" was used to refer to Greenville's crime scene that was reminiscent of the big city's reputation.

The Red Baron's unique German fare was something that Greenville's downtown customers had never been exposed to. Haus Edelweiss (outside of downtown's core on Stone Avenue) wouldn't open for another four years. Marvin was an unlikely restauranteur. According to a *Greenville News* interview, he worked as a systems analyst for Lyman Printing and Finishing Co. in the early days of computer programming but sought to go into business for himself. Beth grew up in Leverkusen, Germany, where her family ran a small restaurant. Beth learned how to cook authentic dishes there and continued to hone her skills while working at Vince Perone's in Greenville. She was well equipped to open her own restaurant when she and her husband committed to opening downtown. However, it almost didn't happen. The couple was ready to move to Columbia, South Carolina, but changed direction when they met Mayor Max Heller. The mayor was several years into his term and faced a daunting situation trying to fix the major problems downtown. Heller grew up in Austria and was captivated by the Hambletons' desire to open a German restaurant. It was just the European touch that Heller wanted to bring a new aesthetic to Main Street. He and Buck Mickel convinced them to stay and open their restaurant here.

The building's exterior was upfitted with stucco white walls accented with dark beams crossing the façade like the front of a Bavarian storefront. Above the doorway was a cartouche with the Red Baron logo. The entryway was distinctive with large wrought-iron gates flanking the outer doorway. The interior was decorated with a collection of more than twelve hundred empty beer cans and German beer steins and an electric train that ran on a track near the ceiling.

Service was lunch only and was in a cafeteria-style model. The Hambletons could interact with each guest while they made their choices of food, and they loved to get to know the regulars. The opening menu served items like sauerbraten (marinated beef roast) and rolladen (beef roulades), but customers were hesitant to try new things. The Hambletons adjusted with more familiar items like wurst and kraut. Since Beth was born in Germany and knew how to cook the authentic dishes, she handled the job as primary cook while Marvin took care of the variety of baked desserts. Over time, more German dishes were added to the menu. Greenville's Octoberfest festival (started by Fritz Mann, Heinrich Looser and their wives) started a year before Red Baron's opened, so there was already an eager crowd ready to patronize the restaurant.

Sandwiches were the most popular menu items and included the following:

The Red Baron: lean corned beef, German style red cabbage, mild curry sauce and melted cheese, served open-faced on rye.
The Big Dolly: all-white turkey breast, lettuce, tomato, special ranch-style sauce and lots of provolone cheese on country grain bread.
The French Connection: all-white turkey breast, imported ham, lettuce, tomato, special sauce, marinated onions and imported Swiss cheese on a giant croissant.
The Bismarck: Smoked German salami and ham topped with marinated onions and melted cheese, served open-faced on French bread.
The Diet Reuben: Turkey, ham, sauerkraut, mild curry sauce and melted cheese, served open-faced on grain bread.

Reuben: Hot lean corned beef, topped with sauerkraut and melted cheese, served open-faced on rye.
German Sampler Plate: smoked Bratwurst with sauerkraut, hot potato salad, red cabbage, bread, and butter.

Soups were also crowd pleasers, with the chicken by George (fresh chicken, vegetables and barley) as the most requested. Other scratch-made soups included mean bean, cream of broccoli, fresh vegetable and beef, beer-cheese and clam chowder.

Marvin was in charge of the desserts, which included German chocolate cheesecake with nuts and cream, chocolate mousse pie with kirsch, Rheinlander cheesecake, carrot cake and marvelous Marvin's magnificent muffins (wild blueberry and butter crunch bran).

A few years after opening, Mayor Heller and the city council put forward plans to reduce Main Street's four-lane Main Street to two, plant trees and widen the sidewalks. Business owners were mixed in their response to the plan, but the Hambletons believed that it could be a good thing for their business. When the $22 million renovations and streetscaping were completed in 1979, it did prove to be good for Red Baron's business.

In 1979, the Red Baron began hosting entertainment events at their restaurant, bringing fun and social events to an otherwise sparse nighttime entertainment scene. One of the early acts was a German band from Spartanburg called the Continentals. In 1981, a local comedy troupe called the And Then Some Players started performing at the restaurant and became a huge hit. The group performed original comedy acts playing off contemporary events, personalities and issues dealing with Greenville. After two years of selling out all one hundred seats for nearly every performance, the group opened its own venue at 101 College Street called Café and Then Some (in 2020, the venue is still running and popular). Though the restaurant's primary act was now gone, the newly created Rebels with Applause comedy troupe took over its spot for a while.

More awareness came to the restaurant that year when the Bavarian Alpine Festival started as an annual event. Business was going well, so in 1984, the Hambletons opened another Red Baron's restaurant in McAlister Square on Pleasantburg Drive. With the new restaurant running, they expanded the menus at both locations, adding items like Weiner Schnitzel (breaded veal cutlet), rolladen and sauerbraten.

Further expansion came in 1990, when the Hambletons opened the Backyard Grill at 120 North Main, just a few doors down from the original restaurant. The new venture, however, broke from the German model and served items like mesquite-grilled hot dogs, hamburgers and chicken sandwiches.

Business continued to go well for the original Red Baron's, and 1997 was the most profitable year of business ever. However, in 1998 the Hambletons' hands were forced to look to retirement when the building that housed their restaurant was purchased by Downtown Investments LLC Caine Co., which planned to renovate the upstairs and add four apartments. To accomplish this and bring the entire building up to code, including the restaurant space, Red Baron's would need to shut down for three or four months. Faced with these circumstances, the couple tried to find a buyer that would keep the restaurant going and purchase the original recipes. That didn't work out, so the popular restaurant closed in 1998, and the Hambletons retired knowing they had been an important part of Greenville's culinary history and early phase of revitalization.

Red Baron's German Potato Salad

6 medium potatoes
6 tablespoons chopped green onions
1 teaspoon salt
¼ teaspoon black pepper
3 tablespoons vegetable oil
¼ cup fried and crumbled bacon
¾ cup water
¼ cup vinegar
1 teaspoon or one cube chicken bouillon
1 tablespoon sugar

In a covered saucepan, cook potatoes until tender. Rinse with cool water and chill for thirty minutes. Peel and slice the potatoes, add onions, salt, pepper, oil and bacon in a large bowl. In a small pan, heat water, vinegar, bouillon and sugar to a boil. Pour over sliced potatoes, mix and serve at room temperature.

German Sweet-Sour Red Cabbage

½ cup diced bacon
1 medium onion, chopped
6 cups shredded red cabbage (about ½ pound)
½ cup applesauce
4 tablespoons sugar
5 cloves
1 tablespoon salt
dash pepper
1 ½ cups water
½ cup white vinegar

Fry bacon until light brown and remove from pan. Sauté onion in bacon fat until glazy but not brown. Add cabbage and all other ingredients, including bacon. Bring to a boil and simmer for twenty minutes, stirring occasionally. More vinegar or sugar may be added to taste.

Viennese Apple Strudel

12½ ounces fine flour
1 egg
pinch salt
1 tablespoon oil
lukewarm water

For filling:
2 ounces butter, melted and divided
2½ ounces breadcrumbs fried in just over 2 ounces butter
4½ pounds apples, peeled and thinly sliced
1 ¾ ounces raisins
cinnamon and sugar

Work the pastry ingredients on a board into a smooth, easy dough. Cover and allow to stand in a warm place for thirty minutes. Spread a large, soft cloth on a table. Dust with flour and roll out the dough. With the floured back of your hand, press the dough, working from the middle outward until it is paper thin. Cut away any thick edges. Brush dough with melted butter and sprinkle with fried breadcrumbs. On the crumbs, place a thick layer of apples, then sprinkle with raisins, cinnamon and sugar. Raise the cloth and roll the pastry up firmly in such a way that the joining line is underneath. Roll it off the cloth and onto a well-buttered baking tin. Brush the strudel with melted butter and bake in a medium oven for thirty minutes until golden brown. During baking, brush occasionally with melted butter. Dust with sugar and serve hot or cold.

Wiener Schnitzel

4 veal cutlets
flour
1 beaten egg
breadcrumbs
salt and pepper
½ cup vegetable oil

Dust cutlets with flour and dip into beaten egg and then breadcrumbs. Add salt and pepper. Pour oil into frying pan and heat. Fry the cutlets for three minutes on each side. Do not overcook. Serve with a lemon wedge.

3
Ryan's Family Steak House

Owners: Alvin McCall Jr.; Buffets, Inc./Ovation Brands
Years open: 1977–2016
Location: 2426 Laurens Road

While this book is meant to feature local, independent restaurants that were part of the fabric of Greenville's culinary history, the importance of Ryan's Family Steak House as the original location of what became a leading national chain is an exception. The story of this remarkable venture begins with Alvin McCall Jr., who grew up in the upstate mill community of Pelzer, South Carolina. His parents worked at the textile mill, and as was common, their large family lived in one of the tract mill houses of the mill village. Just five rooms in the house and one outhouse were shared among the parents and eleven children. Alvin McCall, named after his father, was the ninth child and knew from a very early age how to work hard.

After a successful college education, Alvin landed his first significant job with the Elliott Davis firm but began dabbling in the housing industry by building a few homes. According to a *Greenville News* interview, he found that he enjoyed the business and started the McCall Construction Company, where he would go on to develop familiar Greenville neighborhoods like Heritage Hills, Pelham Estates, Pilgrim Point, Spring Forest, Merrifield Park and Wade Hampton Gardens.

Exterior of the original Ryan's Family Steakhouse on Laurens Road. *From author's collection.*

McCall was always looking to improve and seek new ventures. Inspired by the success of the Ponderosa Steak House, he sought out how he could break into the family-friendly budget restaurant market. Now in his mid-forties, he entered the career that would launch his name and restaurants into the national spotlight. In 1971, McCall's first restaurant was called Western Family Steak House, and it was located at 2119 Wade Hampton Boulevard (occupied by Corona Mexican Restaurant in 2020). Over the next five years, the great response to McCall's model led to eight more locations, and he changed the name to Quincy's. Before taking the concept further afield, he sold the successful restaurants to a company that later became TW Services in Spartanburg.

After five years of learning all aspects of the restaurant business, assessing the strengths and weaknesses of the Western Family Steak House brand and discovering what people wanted, McCall was ready to start another model that he believed would exceed all others. First, he had to settle on a name. Rather than going with something like "McCall's" or another obvious choice, Alvin settled on the somewhat random name of Ryan because of its simplicity and Irish ring.

Now armed with a name, in 1977, he opened Ryan's Family Steak House at 2426 Laurens Road. The space was cavernous, with seating for up to 250 guests. Whereas all of the other budget and mainstream steakhouses cut costs by using cheaper meat cuts, Ryan's used all USDA choice, grain-fed western beef. Furthermore, competitors used frozen meat, while Ryan's used only fresh meat that was brought in and butchered in the restaurant's kitchen. Beyond the great steak selections, the menu had a wide variety of hot and cold entrées, freshly made soups, sides, desserts and a large salad bar. The quality of Ryan's ingredients, the attention to the smallest details of prompt and friendly service and immaculately clean carpets, bathrooms, tables and counter surfaces—all at an affordable price—brought value to a Ryan's experience that beat the competition. And there was plenty of competition in town for the family-friendly budget restaurants. Besides Shoney's, with its large buffet, steakhouses included Western Sizzlin' Steak House, Bonanza Steak House and Jack's Steak House. Ryan's soon rose to the top without any paid advertising in print media, television or radio.

As McCall was ready to expand to his next location on White Horse Road in 1979, he hired Charlie Way to be his controller for expansion. Charlie was a perfect fit and would be a crucial employee in the years to come. By 1981, Ryan's operated six restaurants and took its first foray into the franchising industry by opening a location in Charlotte, North Carolina. Earnings reached just under $1 million that year, and business was on a steady rise. McCall wanted to raise a large amount of capital to finance more restaurants throughout the region, and he took Ryan's public, offering stock options for all employees to be vested in the business. The initial stock offering generated $3.7 million with a value of $9.25 per share; another in 1983 raised $7.7 million, and by the end of 1985, the company had another $5.2 million from stock offerings, ending with thirty-nine restaurants and twelve franchises.

The greatest innovation in the company's history (and one of the biggest in American restaurant history) rolled out in September 1985, with the introduction of the "mega bar." The idea came from Alvin's son T. Mark McCall and was a sixty-four-foot-long U-shaped continuous cornucopia of sixty-eight separate items of food, including barbecued ribs, fried chicken wings, meat loaf, chocolate mousse, banana pudding and seemingly endless salad items. Even in their wildest dreams, Ryan's executives did not anticipate the overwhelming response. The company had its first $1 million sales week while by year's end, sales soared 39.0 percent to $55 million. The closing profit margin for 1985 was 9.9 percent, far outpacing even the McDonald's restaurant chain. The megabar's popularity and profits thrust the company into the national spotlight. Expansion commenced at an unprecedented pace.

As new locations were identified through extensive research, real estate costs and construction were paid in cash. New restaurants had seating capacities of 325 compared to the standard 250 from previous years. Staff were thoroughly trained, and operations were running smoothly before another location was built. Not resting on the laurels of the mega bar's success, the company continued to build on it and innovate by adding an unlimited ice cream bar in 1986—all with no price increase to the customer. Americans increasingly recognized the value of Ryan's quality ingredients, service and affordable price for a tremendous amount of food. Consequently, Ryan's stock became one of the hottest in the country. By the end of 1986, investors who first bought shares in 1982 had realized an increase in value of 2,000 percent.

Ryan's needed a new headquarters and planned for a Greenville location. Due to some parking restrictions on the land, it chose to locate the $2 million facility at 405 Lancaster Avenue in Greer, South Carolina. By 1988, McCall had set his eyes west and brought new locations to Arkansas, Missouri and Iowa. Competitors tried to emulate aspects of the mega bar, but Ryan's continued its upward trajectory. That year, *Forbes* ranked the business as one of the two hundred best small companies in the United States.

As with most companies, the early 1990s were tougher years during the United States' recession and involvement in the Persian Gulf War. Tastes were also shifting, and Ryan's executives sought to break into new markets. With Charlie Way now at the helm after McCall's retirement, the next chapters of Ryan's story unfolded. The company test-marketed a new, casual, alcohol-serving, Tex-Mex dining concept called Chilaca Grille on Greenville's Haywood Road and then in Myrtle Beach. An Italian buffet concept called Bellisimo's was experimented with in Ohio, and a classic western restaurant called Laredo Grille was opened in several Texas cities. While none of these panned out and the company spent millions on the attempts, strong performance from the Ryan's restaurants brought $448.2 million in revenue (up 14 percent from the previous year) in 1994, with a total of 210 company stores and 31 franchises. Further innovations like the all-you-can-eat bakery bar and the division of the previous U-shaped mega bar into six separate "scatter bars" kept customers coming in droves.

By the end of the decade, Ryan's had been named America's favorite steakhouse chain by *Restaurants & Institutions* magazine and marked it's twentieth anniversary with $600 million in sales. The new century brought another innovation with an all-you-can-eat steak feature for the mega bar, and customers responded by increasing sales by 20 percent on the nights it was offered. Charlie Way added a popular feature in the early 2000s by letting customers watch the chefs cook the meats in front of them. Competitors soon followed the lead. In the next few years, the company grew to well over three hundred stores in twenty-one states, with sales reaching more than $800 million.

In 2003, Ryan's vice president of operations Rick Erwin left the company after twenty-three years and went on to lead one of the largest and most successful restaurant groups in Greenville's modern culinary era. The Ryan's company that Alvin McCall built, and Charlie Way continued to expand, was sold to Buffets Inc. (now called Ovation Brands) in 2006. Unable to sustain its predecessor's success, Buffets Inc. went through several rounds of bankruptcy. In 2019, only sixteen Ryan's restaurants remain in operation.

Alvin McCall Jr. died on July 31, 2016, and a week later, the original Ryan's Family Steakhouse at 2426 Laurens Road closed. Though Ryan's founder and the original location are now gone, Greenville, South Carolina, will forever be known as the birthplace of one of the most successful restaurant chains in America.

4
Seven Oaks Restaurant

Owners: Al and Martha Rasche; Kiyohiri and Chigusa Tsuzuki
Years open: 1983–2002
Location: 104 Broadus Avenue

Al and Martha Rasche were very familiar with the grand 1895 Victorian home on Broadus Avenue. They passed it while going to church at Fourth Presbyterian across the street and when visiting Greenville. When the home (originally built by textile mill owner Charles E. Graham) went up for sale in 1981, they jumped on the opportunity and soon settled on the idea of opening a high-end restaurant in the elegant mansion. However, the vine- and wisteria-covered home had suffered neglect and ultimately ran up a renovation bill of more than $1 million.

Al Rasche was a perfectionist and spared no expense to make the venue one that would be first class in every aspect. A new 3,500-square-foot addition was added to house the state-of-the-art kitchen and smokehouse. Original hand-cut rock maple parquet floors and stained-glass windows were restored along with the fireplaces that adorned each room. The basement space that used to store coal for the fireplaces was converted to a wine cellar boasting 130 varieties. The grand ballroom that originally occupied the top floor was made into functional offices. For the dining space, six rooms with fourteen-foot ceilings were decorated with furniture in a late nineteenth century French style and tables covered with white

RESIDENCE OF CHARLES E. GRAHAM.

Left: Charles Graham's house on Broadus Avenue. Graham was an owner of the Huguenot Mill and the Camperdown Mills on the Reedy River. He built this home in the 1890s. *Courtesy of the South Carolina Room, Greenville County Library System.*

Opposite: The grand staircase off the entry hallway is one of the many impressive features of this Victorian home. *From author's collection.*

table clothes. Capacity seating was about 130 guests. These efforts were rewarded the next year when Al Rasche won a Greenville Board of Realtors revitalization award.

Men were required to wear jackets after 6:00 p.m., and when guests arrived, waiters decked out in tuxedos catered to their needs while classical music filled the air. The cuisine was decidedly French with touches of a northern Italian influence, and rightly so, as Executive Chef Robert Plantadis was a classically trained Frenchman, who was perhaps the first chef in Greenville to bring a fully farm-to-table concept to the menu. The *Greenville News* reported that the chef developed relationships with area farmers and took a hands-on roll, instructing the farmers how he wanted the cattle, pigs and chickens to be fed (milk-fed veal and grain-fed beef) and slaughtered to yield the most tender and flavorful meats. When the meat and seafood arrived, he would butcher it himself. Various French breads were baked fresh daily and served to each guest upon arrival.

Dinner entrées that graced the early menu included veal scallopini crustacés en brochette and lobster thermidor. At lunch, guests could choose from such dishes as cannelloni au gratin (all pastas were made in-house as well), poultry supreme and red snapper vesuvio. To finish the experience, desserts, of course, were also made from scratch.

The same year Seven Oaks opened, it participated in Fall for Greenville's Taste of the Town culinary event as one of twenty-three featured eateries. The dishes it offered were lamb chop with mint sauce, fruit tartelettes, chocolate eclairs and coffee vanille. This was only the festival's second year in operation, but it was such a success that attendance doubled from the previous year. The added exposure of thirty thousand people in one weekend was a perfect way to help kick off the new restaurant's placement among the culinary elite of the city.

Hosting elegant and memorable weddings is what put this restaurant in the hearts and memories of so many Greenvillians. The old-world charm of the house and grounds was unique and attracted hundreds of couples to make their lifetime memories there. Beyond hosting regular weddings, many other creative outlets brought their ambiance and cuisine to wide audiences. Chef and manager William Gottsacker took part in ice carving events at the restaurant and in town at the Southern Home and Garden Show. Contemporary fashion was on full display when the restaurant entered into a partnership with the J.B. White Department Store to host its annual spring fashion show. A few years later, a memorable evening of Russian cuisine was presented to the public as a fundraising event for the Greenville Symphony Orchestra.

By 1985, Seven Oaks encountered high-end downtown dining competition from the Commerce Club on the top story of the new U.S. Shelter building. Furthermore, the downtown workforce had grown from 8,500 to 13,000 in the previous four years, forcing Seven Oaks to step up its game. In February, it shut down for a week and rallied locals to "Join the Revolution!" with its new direction toward a more casual American atmosphere. A new manager brought a freshness to the front of house, while a new chef composed a new all-American menu, featuring such dishes as crabmeat sausage with grilled cornbread, filet mignon with trio mushrooms, Pawley's Island steam pot, prime rib, baked salmon Alaska, red snapper almondine and roasted Carolina pheasant, "all at reasonable prices."

In 1988, after five years of the hectic yet rewarding life of running a restaurant, the Rasches decided to move on and sell the restaurant. Kiyohiri Tsuzuki bought Seven Oaks as his first Greenville venture in the food industry (see the Nippon Center Yagoto entry for his next Greenville restaurant). He came from Japan to start a textile mill, TNS Mills, in Blacksburg, South Carolina, in 1967. A few years before acquiring Seven Oaks, Tsuzuki took over one of Buckhead Atlanta's premier fine dining establishments, which was in a restored 1797 antebellum that exuded the same Old South charm that the 1895 Greenville mansion offered. Tsuzuki closed Seven Oaks for two months in 1988 for extensive renovations and painting. New chef Bill McKenzie continued to serve an American-centric menu with favorites that included grilled veal chop with sundried tomatoes, filet mignon, tournados Tazewell II and roast duckling. Soon the restaurant boasted the most extensive wine list in South Carolina, with 160 varieties and two wine cellars.

In the ensuing years, chefs and menus continued to change. In 1994, the most popular entrée was the seafood trio—each item served with its own sauce. Others include roasted rack of lamb in puff pastry with rosemary sauce and chicken "Seven Oaks" with sautéed tarragon and sherry wine sauce topped with cheese and shrimp. Each entrée was served with potatoes or rice, fresh vegetables and homemade bread.

Like the previous owners, the Tsuzukis continued to find creative ways to bring in guests. A series of murder mystery dinners delighted patrons with a combination of great food and drinks, theater and lighthearted comedy. In real life drama, perhaps one of the property's seven oaks being struck by lightning was an omen for the restaurant. As competition grew and tastes changed (a lighter fare and salads were in greater demand), a nineteen-year tradition of dining at Seven Oaks ended in early 2002. The home has been beautifully restored and in 2020 is the home office for Family Legacy financial planning.

Robert's Lamb Chops with Mint Sauce

6 lamb chops
fresh chopped peppermint
fresh chopped spearmint
fresh chopped thyme leaves
1 cup red wine vinegar
8 ounces apple mint jelly

Dredge lamb chops in mint and herb mixture and place in refrigerator for at least two hours. Take more of the mint and thyme leaves and form a bouquet. Drop in a saucepan with one cup of red wine vinegar. Heat and reduce until liquid is gone. Add 8 oz. of apple mint jelly to pan with dried herb leaves and bring to a boil for about fifteen minutes. Pass through a sieve, retaining extracted liquid. Serve hot or cold with lamb chops that have been baked at 450 degrees until desired doneness.

5

Stax's Peppermill

Owners: George, Michael and Chris Stathakis; Stanley and George Coumos
Years open: 1986–2010
Location: 30 Orchard Park Drive

When George Stathakis heard about the $9 million new Haywood Plaza shopping center in 1985, he knew he was ready to expand the family restaurant business. Restaurants had been in his life since childhood when his father owned the Grill Café in his native Greenwood, South Carolina. George worked at various restaurants growing up before joining the navy in 1965. When he returned after service, his parents had moved to Greenville, South Carolina, and George knew of nothing else to pursue other than starting a restaurant.

With the help of a neighbor who was a banker, he took out a loan and opened Dinah's Country Kitchen in partnership with his brother Tommy. The A-frame building was across from Greenville Technical College on Pleasantburg Drive and seemed positioned well for college patrons and suburbia. Without enough capital, the restaurant lasted only half a year. Undaunted, George was determined to get back on his feet, correct his previous mistakes and give it another go. After gaining valuable experience managing Shakey's Pizza and then managing Vince Perone's Spartanburg location, George was ready to start another restaurant with the proper funds and plan. When Shaw's Pharmacy Luncheonette went up for sale in

"Get In The Twosome Habit!"

A New Dining Experience Is In Store For You . . .

OPENING WEDNESDAY APRIL 15th

FEATURING

2—Country Ham & Biscuit Sandwiches	95c
2—Country Sausage & Biscuit Sandwiches	80c
2—Country Fried Steak & Biscuit Sandwiches	95c
2—Large Fried Chicken Breasts with Mashed Potatoes, Gravy & Biscuit	1.20

ALSO

Broiled Corn-on-the-Cob	25c
CUBAN SANDWICH (Salami, Ham, Turkey, Swiss Cheese on A Cuban Loaf)	$1
2—Pork Chops & Biscuit Sandwiches	95c
2—Fish & Biscuit Sandwiches (with tartar sauce)	70c

WITH

MILK SHAKES	SOFT DRINKS	COFFEE, TEA, MILK
29c	15c & 20c	15c

FAST FOOD SERVICE
Eat In or Take Out Service
Plenty of Free Parking
OPEN 7 AM - 10 PM DAILY

DINAH'S COUNTRY KITCHEN

OWNERS: MIKE, TOM & GEORGE STATHAKIS — TEL: 239-2956
501 South Pleasantburg Drive
(Directly Across From Greenville TEC)

Dinah's Country Kitchen on South Pleasantburg Drive was George Stathakis's first restaurant. A succession of nine restaurants under the Stax family brand would follow on the footsteps of this initial venture. *Courtesy of the* Greenville News, USA TODAY NETWORK.

1975, George and his wife, Paula, bought it, did the necessary renovations and turned it into Stax's Restaurant.

In the '70s, breakfast diners and meat-and-threes like Gene's were popular gathering spots for people who lived and worked in nearby neighborhoods. Stax's became a hit with locals, and the hospitality and friendliness of the Stathakis family kept people coming back. George's ambition to open a fine dining restaurant grew in the coming years. Choices for Greenville's fine dining in the early 1980s were limited to a handful of restaurants including the Fishmarket, Vince Perone's, Rib & Loin, Seven Oaks, Ye Olde Fireplace. Only the Fishmarket was anywhere close to the burgeoning area of Haywood Mall, so when Haywood Plaza was announced, George had the capital, experience, location and determination to fulfill his dream.

George sold his interest in Stax's Restaurant to his brother Tommy (who later sold it to his brother Frank, who changed the name to Stax's Original a few years later) and put his resources toward the construction, décor, menu planning and staffing for Stax's Peppermill. George knew he needed a top-notch chef, and applications came from around the country. A few finalists from Atlanta, Washington and Chicago came to cook for George in person. Stanley Coumos previously held prominent positions at well-known restaurants in Chicago, including Hy's of Canada. Stanley's cousin in Greenville, Jimmy Como, encouraged him to apply for the job. Chef Coumos cooked a steak for George, and it was about the best he had ever tasted, so he offered Stanley the job. Coumos was also Greek, and the two got along great. A year after Stanley became the executive chef of Stax's Peppermill, George took him on as partner in the restaurant.

Stax's Peppermill quickly became a local favorite for lunch and dinner and was known especially for the surf and turf. The ambiance and décor were perhaps the nicest around, with white tablecloths in the 160-seat split-level dining area. It also offered forty outdoor seats on the covered patio and private banquet rooms for groups of up to 120. Large Palladian windows bathed rooms with light during lunch, while walls in earth tones featured elegant candleholders, and individually lit tables provided a romantic and relaxing mood for dinner service. Fresh seafood was flown in daily, with gulf shrimp cocktail, baked oysters Rockefeller, iced king crab cocktail, escargot, marinated herring, Nova Scotia salmon and Saganaki flambé featured

George Stathakis and wife, Paula, inside Stax's Peppermill. *Courtesy of George Stathakis.*

on the appetizer menu. Entrées included scallops à la George, filet of red snapper, whole sea bass, trout Coumos, broiled West Coast salmon steak and fresh Florida grouper. Six to ten fresh fish options were offered daily and could include cobia, shark, tuna, red fish, stone crabs, swordfish, mahi mahi, wahoo, trigger fish, halibut, turbot and sturgeon. Each of these were bought as whole fish and butchered in house into large dinner portions. When asked what dish he was most proud of, George replied that the fried lobster tail was it. Though seemingly a straightforward dish, he and Chef Stanley traveled to Atlanta to learn the nuances and secrets of preparation and cooking, which set their version apart from any in town.

Certified prime beef makes up less than 1 percent of all beef sold in the United States, and Stax's Peppermill was the first to offer it daily and exclusively on its menu. A wide range of choices for this prize meat included rib-eye, T-bone, filet mignon, sirloin steak, New York strip and steak Neptune. Beyond the high-quality entrées, top-notch service was taught, expected and delivered at Stax's Peppermill. Dishes like the steak Diane, Dover sole meunière and veal piccata had the entertainment aspect of being cooked tableside. Other popular dishes ranged from the Athenian breast of chicken and rack of lamb to the chateaubriand or tournedos Rossini. Formally attired waitstaff served tables in teams—one took orders, one promptly delivered the food and one refilled drinks, bread and fulfilled other requests.

George was present for both lunch and dinner service all week, greeting many guests by name and visiting tables to see how everyone was enjoying the experience. Further personal attention was afforded with tableside cooking if guests ordered the baked Alaska, cherries jubilee or bananas foster from the dessert menu. The bananas foster had a particular wow factor. When the chef stealthily threw cinnamon into the flaming dessert, it sparkled and crackled to the customers' delight.

After two years of great success, George and Stanley pursued another opportunity by opening a "big city" type of diner called Stax Omega next door at 72 Orchard Park Drive. The concept was modeled on a diner of the same name, Omega, in Chicago that George and Stanley thought would be a great addition to the city's culinary scene. Within a year, they expanded the footprint and opened Stax's International Bakery next door to Stax Omega. While Stax's Peppermill catered to the business class, special occasion and higher-end clientele, George explained in a *Greenville News* interview that Omega was branded as family restaurant where "people could get anything they wanted any time of day without a bar atmosphere."

A third restaurant under Stathakis and Coumos, called Stax's Grill, opened in the late summer of 1990 at 850 Woods Crossing Road. It was meant to hit the market between Omega and Peppermill. George's cousin Charlie Cavalaris was brought on as a partner in the grill, and it was later owned by George's son Chris. Having restaurants with lower price points was fortuitous, as the United States would enter in a recession that same year. As high-end restaurants struggled to maintain steady numbers, Stax's Peppermill remained steady.

In an effort to promote independently owned restaurants and foster closer comradery between owners, George spearheaded a new organization. Stax's Peppermill banded together with fifteen other independently owned fine dining restaurants to form Greenville's distinctive restaurant association, known as the Blue Plate Society. Membership offered customers great incentives to continue regularly dining out, with a value that could reach more than $1,000. Benefits allowed guests to have forty-eight free dinners (three coupons per restaurant). Customers responded and soon Stax's Peppermill was voted as the best all-around restaurant in the Best of the Upstate awards—a designation that would be held for many years to come. Mobil awarded another accolade with a prestigious three-star rating.

Having weathered the recession, George and Stanley embarked on a new venture in 1991, mass producing and marketing their special blends of seasonings. Their seasoning salt, all-purpose, Greek and rotisserie seasonings started out locally but ultimately became available in stores nationwide. Restaurant expansion continued in 1992, with George and Stanley's acquisition of the former Braden's Restaurant in Anderson, which they renamed Stax's of Anderson. George's contributions to Greenville's community were recognized by the chamber of commerce the next year when he was named the small businessperson of the year. By then, George's restaurants were also receiving national attention, and they collectively won five of the nation's highest restaurant awards, with rankings in the top two hundred each time.

In the mid-1990s, a piano bar was added to the Peppermill's dining space and became very popular. Initially, Joe Langley and his band entertained guests on Thursday and Friday evenings with no cover charge. In the late '90s, Dwight Woods became a regular pianist at the piano bar.

Further business expansion came in the '90s when Stax's Carolina Roasters opened at the Haywood Mall food court and Stax's Boiler Room opened across from the Hyatt Regency hotel downtown. A full-service catering operation rounded out the growing company's portfolio in 1997.

Interior of the Peppermill with its custom serpentine bar after the $1 million renovation in 2004. *Courtesy of George Stathakis.*

After attending culinary school at Johnson & Wales and then helping Brennan's chef Mike Roussel in various New Orleans cooking shows, George's son Michael Stathakis became the executive sous chef at Brennan's. Equipped with this valuable training and experience, Michael returned to Greenville to become chef under the training of Stanley Coumos. Using the experience that he gained in New Orleans, Michael started the *Cooking with Stax's* television show on Greenville's Fox channel in 1998. He was the first in the Southeast (beating the large Atlanta and Charlotte markets) to do a regional cooking show. The show reached 750,000 households and ran from 1998 to 2009, with 185 episodes. Stanley's son, George Coumos, returned from college with a business degree around this time to work at Stax's Peppermill.

In 2004, with the second-generation of George Coumos and Michael Stathakis in charge of daily operations, Stax's Peppermill underwent a $1 million renovation and a name change to the Peppermill. Some factors that brought about the need for change included increased fine dining competition from Greenville's downtown restaurants and the proliferation of national chains (like Outback Steakhouse just across the street). The partners thought a face-lift could communicate a more casual feel than the traditionally formal space. When guests arrived, the beautifully crafted serpentine bar was the first indication of the new cosmopolitan look. A creative cocktail or wine could be ordered there along with an Asian-inspired bar menu headed by sushi chef Akira Matsumura. Guests enjoyed such items as his wide array of sushi and sashimi creations, a sumo Kobe burger or a blackened salmon filet.

After one of the owners greeted and seated guests, a flavorful cheese-coated bread freshly baked next door at Stax's International Bakery got the taste buds going. Chuck Hanford continued to serve as the head chef, and one of the most talked-about appetizers was the seafood tower, consisting of an impressively stacked array of oysters, shrimp, lump crab, ahi tuna, nori rolls and 1.25 pounds of lobster. Along with steak selections from the previous menu, American Kobe steak could now be found as another great option. A more exotic addition was the ostrich with black truffle and foie gras terrine. Beyond these fancier options, a lower price point was found across the menu, with entrées now starting at $14.95. The same year that the Peppermill took on these changes, the partners opened a second location of Stax Omega (called Omega 2) across from Michelin's headquarters near Pelham Road and I-85.

According to George Stathakis, as the first decade of the new century came to a close, he and Stanley shared thoughts of selling off their interests in the business. Ultimately, George decided to sell his stake to Stanley and enjoy a well-deserved retirement after a forty-year restaurant career. A few months later, the Coumoses closed the Peppermill and Omega 2, ending a nearly twenty-five-year chapter in the Stathakis and Coumos family business. As of 2020, the legacy of the families continues to serve multiple generations in the community through Stax's Original, Stax Omega, Stax's International Bakery and Stax's Catering.

Stax's Peppermill Bananas Foster Recipe

¼ cup (½ stick) butter
1 cup brown sugar
½ teaspoon cinnamon
¼ cup banana liqueur
4 bananas, cut in half lengthwise, then halved
4 scoops vanilla ice cream

Combine the butter, sugar and cinnamon in a flambé pan or skillet. Place the pan over low heat and cook, stirring, until the sugar dissolves. Stir in the banana liqueur, then place the bananas in the pan. Continue cooking until sauce is hot and bananas soften and begin to brown. Lift the bananas out of the pan and place four pieces over each portion of ice cream. Generously spoon warm sauce over the top of the ice cream and serve immediately.

6
The Fishmarket

Owners: Rene Rott and Martin Dobr
Years open: 1980–88
Location: 3715 East North Street, Loehmann's Plaza

The two men behind the Fishmarket had quite an adventurous life journey before coming to Greenville, South Carolina, to open their restaurant in 1980. Rene Rott and Martin Dobr were born in war-torn Prague, Czechoslovakia (now Czech Republic). Rene became an accomplished professional soccer player, and Martin pursued a successful career in cooking. Their paths crossed while attending the Czechoslovakian Hotel and Restaurant School, and the pair became close friends. Russia invaded their country in 1968, and within a few months, Rene and Martin had fled the country saying they were merely going to vacation in Austria. The "vacation" was a six-week stay at a refugee camp.

Unwilling to wait for the required year to enter America, the pair went to Ottawa, Canada. Dobr landed a job working for Canada's prime minister before moving to a chef position in Los Angeles, California. Rott got a beverage director position at a Canadian hotel before moving to various U.S. cities and eventually ending up in California. There he teamed up with his friend Dobr again and opened their first restaurant venture called Checkers Restaurant. After catering to Hollywood movie stars and celebrities, Dobr visited his parents in Greenville and saw a need for fine dining. He brought

Advertisement for the Fishmarket. *Courtesy of the* Greenville News, USA TODAY NETWORK.

Dobr on to open the Fishmarket in Loehmann's Plaza at the corner of Howell and East North Streets.

They had become experts in the procurement and cooking techniques of fresh fish in Hawaii, so the Czech friends chose seafood as the specialty of their Greenville location. The men advertised themselves as the "only seafood restaurant in Greenville" and even "Carolina's only seafood restaurant." Linen table clothes, mounted game fish décor, a stone fireplace, aquariums, a large wine list and nightly live piano music brought a level of fine dining and ambiance that Greenville patrons craved. Baked salmon, stuffed scrod and broiled swordfish became quick guest favorites, but the extensive seafood menu also included choices of live Maine lobster, soft shell crab, sautéed grouper, trout, filet of sole, shrimp scampi, scallops, clam chowder, bouillabaisse à la Maison and cioppino Fishmarket style. Meat selections included veal piccata, chicken breast parmigiana, filet mignon, lamb chops calabrese and frog legs.

After three years in Greenville, Rott left to open similar Fishmarket concepts in Charlotte, North Carolina, and Boca Raton, Florida. Meanwhile, Chef Dobr continued to dazzle guests with his seafood lunch and dinner selections.

Fishmarket co-owner Rene Rott and his mother inside the restaurant's dining room. *Courtesy of the South Carolina Room, Greenville County Library System.*

In 1986, Chef Dobr hired his daughter's boyfriend Tyler to wash dishes. Tyler soaked in the atmosphere, hospitality going on in the restaurant and high level of cooking in the kitchen. He was enamored of the energy and techniques he saw and worked his way into a prep cook position, followed quickly by a promotion to line cook. While Tyler's trajectory through kitchen positions was somewhat common, the spark for the love of food, cooking and hospitality at the Fishmarket would lead him to a lifelong career with uncommon results.

After moving on to cooking school at Johnson & Wales in Charleston, South Carolina, Tyler Florence made his way to New York City and took a successful bite out of the Big Apple's culinary scene. After early gigs at Aureole and Mad 61, Florence worked his way up to executive chef at Cafeteria. It was around this time that a new food television concept was taking off, Food Network. The executives recognized Tyler's talent and personality and gave him his first hosting job on *Food 911*. His charm and cooking knowledge were a hit with viewers, leading to further hosting jobs like *How to Boil Water*, *Tyler's Ultimate* and the *Great Food Truck Race*.

By 1988, the Dobrs were struggling to maintain a steady stream of guests in what was considered an expensive restaurant at the time. By then, competition had grown throughout town, notably with the fresh seafood flown in daily down the street at Stax's Peppermill. Consequently, they closed the Fishmarket and reopened it that year with a more casual and less expensive concept, calling it the East Side Oyster Bar and Grill. Seafood remained the focus but at a different price point. Fishmarket meals could easily cost between $40.00 and $50.00, but the Oyster Bar offered dishes in the range of $4.00 to $26.00. Entrées were named after familiar east side streets, like the knolls of Pelham calamari, Inglewood she crab soup, Botany Arms stuffed mushrooms, Sugar Mill T-Bone, Devenger mixed grill, Merrifield Park shrimp and sausage and a chopped salad with bacon, chicken and blue cheese called Wellington green salad. It even offered $4.95 country specials like liver and onions and baked chicken breasts.

Chef Dobr left the Oyster Bar—and his Italian Market Restaurant around the corner—after about a year and moved to Myrtle Beach, where he opened a successful fine dining restaurant called Martin's. Rene Rott ended up coming back to open Rene's Fish Market near Haywood Mall in 1992 and later started the successful Rene's Steak House in the old coach factory building (Wyche Pavilion) in the Peace Center complex in 1999.

PART IV

1990–2015: FOUNDATIONS FOR A MODERN CULINARY SCENE

WITH A PLAN FOR THE FUTURE AND AN UPDATED AESTHETIC of Main Street already in place by 1990, the primary elements Greenville needed to continue its revitalization were to get people to live, work and play downtown. At the start of the decade, one of the key components of Greenville's revitalization came into place—the opening of the $42 million Peace Center for the Performing Arts complex. Eight years earlier, the Hyatt Regency opened as an anchor on the far end of North Main. The Peace Center was located on the Reedy River at the southernmost part of Main Street before going into the West End. It became the second major anchor bringing locals and visitors into downtown. The 2,100-seat concert hall immediately brought in top-notch performances, beginning with the Broadway smash *CATS*. Beyond the Broadway series, the facility hosted a steady lineup of musicians, comedians and other performers. The Greenville Symphony Orchestra's season of events provided more exciting reasons to travel downtown. Thousands of people began going downtown on a regular basis. However, their choices for dining before and after performances were few.

While the preceding downtown improvements were crucial, the Peace Center was the true spark that ignited the modern culinary scene in Greenville's downtown. Existing restaurants had a growing base of steady customers and opening a new restaurant became a much more attractive prospect for entrepreneurs. More European-style restaurants opened, like Rose-Marie's Café (French), Henni's German Restaurant and Bistro Europa, which were also the first to put dining tables on the sidewalk—a trend that would ultimately help define the vibe of the downtown dining experience. The 858 brought in a Culinary Institute of America–trained chef from Atlanta to lead the way for modern plating and presentation.

Outside of downtown, the Nippon Center Yagoto added a truly immersive international experience with Japanese authenticity that extended through the food, drinks, staff, chefs, building and materials, décor, landscaping/grounds, service-ware and ceremonial events.

Greenville's first James Beard Award–nominated chef arrived in 2002 at the unpretentious 33 Liberty Restaurant off South Pleasantburg Drive in the Pleasantburg Shopping Center. Chef John Malik came to Greenville from New Orleans and cooked an array of flavor profiles and sophisticated dishes that caught the attention of local foodies and national food writers. Restaurant O brought a level of sophisticated contemporary cuisine and ambiance that was previously unknown. And American Grocery Restaurant took a pioneering role in starting a true farm-to-table restaurant, supper club dinners and a craft cocktail program that led to the city's first speakeasy.

1
33 Liberty Restaurant

Owners: John and Amy Malik
Years open: 2001–2008
Location: 33 Liberty Lane

The story of 33 Liberty and its owners is one of most the interesting and important in the early stages of Greenville's modern culinary scene, yet many locals might not be familiar with it. There are two main reasons for this. One is that it was in a somewhat obscure strip mall outside of downtown on a part of Pleasantburg Drive that was less popular than it had been in the 1960s through the '80s (when nearby Vince Perone's was in its heyday). The other reason is that its fine dining menu was expensive. Nonetheless, 33 Liberty made significant strides in putting Greenville on the Southeast's culinary radar.

The owners, John and Amy Malik, received their training in one of America's great culinary destinations, New Orleans. John was born there, but Amy moved from Memphis; they met after enrolling in the culinary apprenticeship program at Delgado Community College. Both worked at the French/Creole Christian's Restaurant, and John later worked under Chef Daniel Bonnot at the Restaurant de la Tour Eiffel.

The couple made their way to Charleston, where the culinary scene was promising but not yet in the national spotlight. The couple's first venture was taking over as proprietors of the Guild Inn (later the Old Village Post House)

Chef John Malik. *From author's collection.*

and as chefs of the associated Supper at Seven Restaurant. After two years, they moved on, and John ended up as executive sous chef at the Mill House Hotel in the heart of Charleston.

A move to Greenville, South Carolina, in 1993 brought John to the Augusta Grill, where he spent five years leading the kitchen. A few years into the job, John realized that he kept reading about the same six or seven chefs who were in the national spotlight. He recognized that they were all focusing on cuisines and ingredients that were from their local areas, making dishes that stood out for their creativity and flavor profiles. Taking their cue, Chef Malik began transforming the products and menus that represented his kitchen. He went out to local farmers and built relationships with people like Chris Sermons at Bio Way Farms, who provided local produce. His outlook was energized, and his cuisine started turning heads in the community. Food industry professionals also took notice. John was invited to cook for a guest chef dinner at Draeger's Grocery in San Mateo, California, and impressed the attendees. One of them worked for the Food Network and hired John to be a guest chef on five episodes of the television show *Ready, Set, Cook*. That led to four episodes appearing on Sara Moulton's show *Cooking Live Primetime* and an appearance on *Door Knock Dinners*. This exposure led to an invitation for Chef Malik to cook at the James Beard House in New York City, something no chef from Greenville had ever done.

John continued to cook at the Augusta Grill through October 1999 but had an experience earlier that year that led him and Amy to their next career move. Chef Michel Richard was one of the top chefs in the United States, and John was able to spend a day with him for a stage at his famed Citronelle Restaurant in Washington, D.C. Rather than training in the kitchen and cooking for the restaurant all day, Chef Richard gave John a tour and carefully explained how things worked there. At the end of the day, John was treated to one of the most amazing culinary experiences he ever had— all served at the restaurant's custom chef's table. John was blown away, and Chef Richard encouraged him to open his own restaurant. John and Amy began planning for a high-end catering business that would fill the demand for Greenville's growing corporate and elite community.

The Maliks started Culinary Capers Catering in a small former pizza shop at 33 Liberty Lane. Business did well, and within a year, patrons were smitten with their cuisine and clamored that they serve dinner on a regular basis. Some tables were set up, and they started serving dinner three nights a week. In 2001, catering was put aside, and the name was changed to 33 Liberty Restaurant. With John as executive chef cooking the entrées and

Dining room of 33 Liberty Restaurant. *Courtesy of John Malik.*

appetizers, Amy continued using her baking talents as pastry chef in charge of all desserts. Tony Keely stayed on from the catering operation and was an additional chef in the kitchen.

As one of the pioneering Greenville chefs using a farm-to-table philosophy, John's menu changed weekly based on the products that the local farms could provide. Guests were treated to courses of food that were equally creative in their ingredient pairings as they were in the complexity of their flavor profiles. According to John, the menu reflected "global, old-world comfort food with southern hospitality with an emphasis on American, French and Italian cuisines." Some examples of the hot appetizers include cheddar cheese biscuits with rabbit confit, pecan smoked duck breast with molasses vinegar and thyme dumplings, and sweet potato blini with pulled pork. A cold appetizer might be crab salad with chive oil, yellow tomato jam and sourdough croutons. Entrées varied widely with seafood, white and red meats and wild game dishes. Some favorites included crab cakes with braised fennel, leeks and sherry beurre blanc, duck breast on a sweet potato fritter with roasted endive and green peppercorn sauce, crawfish risotto with tomato jam and fried quail, buttermilk fried chicken with cane vinegar potato salad and grilled squash and grilled Atlantic swordfish over farmer's market succotash with roasted sweet pepper salsa.

Amy's highly crafted desserts were the perfect ending and included variations of her light and fluffy cheesecake, autumn fruit cobbler with cinnamon ice cream, white chocolate crème brûlée and her signature chocolate torte with white chocolate mousse and caramelized bananas.

In 2003, John dined at a James Beard dinner at the Four Seasons Hotel in Atlanta. Following the event, he was treated to an inspiring dinner at the restaurant's chef's table. When he arrived back home, he immediately created a chef's table space in the kitchen for guests to enjoy the experience in Greenville for the first time. The concept was a hit and attracted scores of people wanting to get behind the scenes and have a close-up interaction with the chefs as they made and served the creative courses. For the chef's tasting menu, guests were never given a printed list of courses. Anticipation built as the inventive dishes were assembled, explained and served. Greenville's modern culinary scene took another step forward.

It didn't take long for word to get around locally, regionally and nationally about the level of food the Maliks were offering. Big business owners and corporate executives from the local BMW plant and Michelin headquarters became frequent customers. For his prowess with house-smoking items like salmon, trout, garlic, tomatoes and pork, John was named to *Bon Appetit's* "Who's Who in American Barbecue" list. A Michelin executive who was a regular guest connected the chef with the BF Goodrich branch, and John began a recurring role cooking various game meats on the television show *BF Goodrich Outdoors* on Fox Sports South. Most of the episodes were filmed at 33 Liberty and all were broadcast to 10.5 million homes in the Southeast. *Bon Appetit's* Barbara Fairchild invited John to cook with some of the best chefs in the United States, including Ben Pollinger of Oceana in New York City, Nancy Oakes of Boulevard in San Francisco and Robert del Grande of Café Annie in Houston, at the 2003 Epicurean Evening to benefit UCLA's Jonsson Cancer Center. For four consecutive years, Disney invited John and Amy to be guest chefs at Epcot International Food and Wine Festival. Amy's dessert talents brought her to participate in the New York Chocolate Show, and soon their restaurant caught the attention of *Southern Living*.

The culmination of John's career as chef and owner of 33 Liberty came in 2008. The Lee Bros. (Matt and Ted Lee) visited Greenville on a book-signing tour and asked to eat at the Maliks' restaurant. After being treating to a memorable meal, Matt Lee recommended John for consideration in one of the highest awards an American chef can receive. Soon, John Malik was recognized as a James Beard nominee for best chef in the Southeast. It was a pioneering achievement for any Greenville chef at that time.

Just as 33 Liberty and its chefs were hitting their stride, the United States plummeted into a recession that devastated many fine dining restaurants. The recession left revenues too low to recover, so the Maliks made the hard decision to close in November 2008. A delicious taste of the restaurant may continue to be enjoyed with the following recipe.

❖❖❖

Amy's Chocolate Torte with White Chocolate Mousse and Caramelized Bananas

Bittersweet Brownie Layer:
1 ounce bittersweet chocolate
2 ounces unsweetened chocolate
¼ cup butter
2 whole eggs
¾ cup sugar
2 teaspoons vanilla
½ cup cake flour

Spray a nine-inch cake pan with nonstick spray and line the bottom with parchment paper circles to fit. Coat parchment lining with flour and shake out excess. Combine chocolate and butter in the top of a double boiler. Gently melt over slowly simmering water, stirring to ensure butter and chocolate are combined. Remove from heat and allow chocolate to cool to room temperature. In another bowl, whip eggs and sugar until fluffy and add vanilla. Slowly add melted chocolate and mix. Sift ½ cup cake flour over batter, using a spatula to gently fold in flour until batter is uniform. Pour batter into cake pan and bake at 350 degrees for twenty minutes. To test doneness, insert a small knife into center. It should come out clean. Cool on rack for ten minutes then remove from pan.

White Chocolate Mousse:
12 ounces white chocolate, chips or chopped
1½ cups heavy cream
3 egg whites

Melt white chocolate and ¾ cup heavy cream in a double boiler, stirring to combine. Remove from heat and set to cool. Whip remaining ¾ cup of heavy cream and transfer to a medium mixing bowl and chill. Do not begin the next step until chocolate mixture is no longer warm to the touch. White chocolate must be liquid but cannot be warm. Whip egg whites in a clean, dry mixing bowl. Whip to stiff peaks. Gently fold egg whites into the chocolate mixture, incorporating completely. Gently fold whipped cream into chocolate and whites until uniform in color. Store mousse in refrigerator until ready to assemble.

Bittersweet Chocolate Sauce:
¼ cup unsweetened cocoa
½ cup sugar
½ cup water
2 ounces bittersweet chocolate

Sift cocoa powder and sugar to combine. Mix remaining ingredients with sugar and cocoa in a one-quart saucepan and heat on medium until sauce comes to a slight boil and is smooth. Set aside to cool.

Caramelized Bananas:
juice from ½ lemon
½ cup sugar
3–4 ripe bananas

Peel and slice bananas into ½ inch thick pieces. Toss in lemon juice to coat. Place sugar in a bowl near stovetop. Heat medium sauté pan over medium heat. To test, drop in a few sugar crystals. If they sizzle, the pan is hot enough. Toss banana slices in sugar and place on flat side in pan. When sugar starts to caramelize, quickly turn bananas to coat the other side. Let cool before placing on mousse.

Dessert Assembly:
Use a nine-inch springform pan as a mold. Place brownie layer in the bottom, trimming sides if necessary. Cover top with white chocolate mousse (up to ½ inch from top). Arrange caramelized bananas over top. Drizzle chocolate sauce on top.

2

American Grocery Restaurant

Owners: Joe and Darlene Clarke; David Sundeen Jr. and Susan Dunmeyer
Years open: 2007–17
Location: 732 South Main Street

The four original owners of American Grocery Restaurant (AGR) met in Los Angeles, but the three chefs, Joe Clarke, David Sundeen Jr. and Susan Dunmeyer, all trained at the French Culinary Institute in New York. Joe and his wife, Darlene, ended up working at a farm-to-table restaurant in Los Angeles called Table 8. That is where they met David and his wife, Susan. Joe and David studied the classic French techniques of cooking, while Susan concentrated on pastries. Darlene, a certified sommelier, excelled at pairing wine with fine cuisine. All four shared a passion for the local-sourcing style of the restaurant but longed to have a place to call their own. They looked to the Southeast, where the farm-to-table model was still in its infancy.

For about a year, the four researched for the best location to start their restaurant. On the short list was Wilmington and Charlotte in North Carolina and Charleston, Columbia and Greenville in South Carolina. The Clarkes were familiar with the upstate of South Carolina, as Joe grew up in Spartanburg and Darlene grew up in Greenwood. Though coming home was a nice perk, the potential of Greenville's culinary scene in 2006 made it a clear choice for several other reasons. Greenville's downtown was one of the most up-and-coming tourist destinations in the South,

Exterior of American Grocery Restaurant. *From author's collection.*

The dining room of American Grocery. *From author's collection.*

with a vibrant Main Street dotted with renovated buildings, museums, theaters, shops and plenty of restaurants. The opening of the Reedy River Falls Park bordering the city's West End Historic District made the area a hotspot for entrepreneurs. Many of the buildings had age, charm and, most importantly, reasonable lease rates—especially compared to the spaces in the North Main section.

In the mid-1990s and early 2000s, Greenvillians were introduced to menus with products sourced from local farmers at a few places like Bistro Europa and 33 Liberty. However, there wasn't a restaurant that billed itself as a farm-to-table destination as the guiding concept of the establishment.

Though sourcing food from an immediate surrounding area was the American norm for centuries, the takeover of processed foods in the early twentieth century triggered a movement away from farms. Then, in the mid-twentieth century, as research on pesticides became available, progressive chefs began to return to civilization's culinary roots, choosing fruits, meats and vegetables that were found as near to the restaurant as possible. Chez Panisse, which opened in 1971 in Berkley, California, is often cited as the pioneer, and the movement later spread to other cities in California, Washington and Colorado. According to Cinnamon Janzer's article "The History of the Farm to Table Movement" in *Upserve Restaurant Insider*, principals guiding the culinary philosophy include using products that are grown, raised and/or retailed in proximity to the restaurant (with lowest environmental impact), sensitivity to the food needs of the larger community, promotion of neighborhoods that can support their own food needs and developing sustainability for communities to maintain their own food needs while enabling future generations to continue using those resources.

In Greenville, Sundeen, Dunmeyer and the Clarkes settled on American Grocery Restaurant as the name for their own farm-to-table venture. With an emphasis on getting products from the upstate of South Carolina, America was their grocery store. Surprisingly, in 2006, there were few farms supplying Greenville's downtown restaurants, so relationships and delivery models needed to be worked out. Joe and David made regular trips to the countryside to meet the growers, find out what products they were planting and set up schedules for harvest.

Jeff Isbell at Iszy's Heirloom Veggies in Liberty, South Carolina, was one of the early suppliers. Arlene and Dean Goforth from Blue Chip Farms & Processing were suppliers from Fountain Inn who hand delivered their rabbits to the chefs at the restaurant. Seafood was brought in freshly caught from the South Carolina coast. When they started, the State of South Carolina had not yet created its Certified South Carolina Grown program. That launched in 2007 and brought farmers, processors, wholesalers, retailers and the South Carolina Department of Agriculture together to brand and promote produces grown in the state. When that was put in place, it was much easier to identify and buy South Carolina products. Over time, many partnerships for the restaurant's grocery list formed, including:

Milk and butter
- Happy Cow Creamery, South Carolina

Vegetables
- Parson's Produce, South Carolina
- Mush Creak Farm, South Carolina
- Greenbriar Farms, South Carolina
- Brannon Morris Micros, South Carolina
- Bio Way Farms, South Carolina

Fish
- Abundant Seafood (Mark Mahefka), South Carolina
- Sunburst Trout Company, South Carolina

Pork
- Caw Caw Creek, South Carolina
- Greenbriar Farms, South Carolina

Lamb
- Greenbriar Farms, South Carolina

Poultry
- Manchester Farms, South Carolina
- Palmetto Pigeon Farm, South Carolina

Eggs
- Merciful Heart Farm, South Carolina

Cheese
- Split Creek Farms, South Carolina
- Sweet Grass Dairy, Georgia

Fruit
- Perdue Mountain Fruit Farm, South Carolina
- Stewart Farm, South Carolina
- McBee Farms, South Carolina
- Gentry Farm, South Carolina

Flour
- Adluh Mills, South Carolina

Grits, Grains and Rice
- Anson Mills, South Carolina

Coffee
- Leopard Forest Coffee Co., South Carolina

The menu was advertised as "refined American seasonal cuisine." Fresh ingredients at the peak of their growing season dictated what would be offered on the weekly changing menu. A sense of culinary adventure and risk-taking were part of the approach.

Snacks featured an array of small plates to order at the bar or at your table to get things going. A basket of house-made fresh breads was served with seasonal jam and freshly churned butter. The sriracha-honey fried chicken skins and fried deviled eggs were choices the customers consistently raved about.

Starters were a particularly great chance for local vegetables to shine. The summer salad consisted of watermelon, white cucumbers, heirloom tomatoes, jalapeño, mint, cilantro, basil and green onion with a lime-chile vinaigrette. Spring vegetable primavera featured goat cheese gnocchi, parmesan and pancetta with fresh basil. A particularly out-of-the-box creation was the grilled lamb heart with hummus and piquillo, shallot jam, grilled spring onion and spiced chickpeas. Other crowd-pleasing appetizers included the charred octopus served over greens with flatbread, salsa verde and toasted almonds; beef albondigas with grits, red chile, cilantro cream and pepitas; veal sweetbreads with pasta primavera and spring peas; crispy veal sweetbread with a Johnny cake, red-wine-braised cabbage, butternut squash hash and applesauce; and the goat cheese gnudi with blueberries, cipollini onion and brown butter.

The house-made charcuterie selections impressed and featured smoked trout pâté with grilled bread; country pate with local pork, rabbit liver and dried cherries; grilled bologna; rabbit liver mousse; and potte rabbit rillette. Artisanal cheese ranged from a five-year Dutch Gouda with saba to the Valdeón blue cheese with pear mostarda to a Deer Creek "Vat 17" cheddar with bourbon cherries and a Blue Ridge Creamery "Jocassee Tomme" with strawberry.

For main entrées, selections might include a Palmetto Farms chicken with sweet potato hash and mushroom ragout; potato-crusted mountain trout with braised kale and crispy leeks; confit of local rabbit with baby carrots, house-made gnocchi, wild mushrooms, arugula and sauce moutarde; salt-crusted Brasstown beef grass-fed ribeye steak with pomme purée, onion soubise and red wine jus; unstuffed flounder, crab, preserved lemon South Carolina golden rice and roquette purée; pork "en veil," creamy fine grits, mustard greens and smoked ham hock broth; and duck breast with lima beans, corn and carrots. The most popular entrée was the braised beef tongue with horseradish gnocchi (or sometimes charred onion spaetzle), arugula and pickled mustard seeds over a smoked tomato creme.

Creative desserts included the house-made doughnuts with lemon pastry crème and buttermilk glaze and the pear upside-down cake with chai ice cream, spiced walnuts and a ginger-balsamic gastrique. For those wanting a full experience, the five-course chef's tasting menu combined many elements of the above items.

STARTERS

MUSSELS — 11. ◊
smoked paprika cream, grilled bread

SPRING VEGETABLE PRIMAVERA — 13.
goat cheese gnocchi, parmesan, pancetta, basil

CHARRED OCTOPUS — 14. ◊
marinated gigande beans, flatbread, romesco, salsa verde, toasted almonds

CORN RAVIOLI — 14.
pork croquettes, corn velouté, tomato jam, basil oil

*GRILLED QUAIL BREAST — 14. ◊
panisse, pickled blueberry gastrique, quail egg, pea tendrils

GRILLED LAMB HEART — 13. ◊
hummus, piquillo – shallot jam, grilled spring onion, spiced chickpeas

GOAT CHEESE GNUDI — 13.
blueberries, cipollini onion, brown butter

SALADS

SPRING GREENS — 11. ◊
marinated blackberries, pickled shitakes, pistachios, radish, spring onion vinaigrette

GRILLED ROMAINE CAESAR — 10.
parmesan, croutons

ENTRÉES

PAN ROASTED GROUPER — 32. ◊
mushroom cream, grilled asparagus, green garlic vinaigrette

SUNBURST TROUT — 29.
chorizo – potato paella, collard greens, lemon aioli, smoked almond aillade

CONFIT OF LOCAL RABBIT — 29.
bacon lardons, spring vegetable ragoût

BRAISED BEEF TONGUE — 28.
charred onion spaetzle, smoked tomato cream

*SALT CRUSTED BRASSTOWN BEEF GRASS-FED RIBEYE STEAK — 46. ◊
pomme purée, onion soubise, red wine jus

CHEF'S SELECTION OF COMPOSED LOCAL VEGETABLES — 26. ◊

SNACKS

DAILY HOUSE MADE BREAD BASKET — 4
seasonal jam, happy cow butter

SRIRACHA-HONEY FRIED CHICKEN SKINS — 5.

FRIED DEVILED EGG — 3.

PIMENTO CHEESE — 5.
house made crackers

CRISPY BRUSSELS SPROUTS — 9. ◊
red wine – cherry gastrique, house made bacon

BUTTERMILK-CHIVE BISCUITS — 5. (add bacon jam — 1.)
*baked to order, please allow up to 15 minutes for preparation

CHARCUTERIE & CHEESE with accompaniments — 12.
(Choose one cheese and one charcuterie; additional are 3. each, unless noted)

HOUSE MADE CHARCUTERIE
grilled bread, grainy mustard & house pickles

Smoked Trout Paté ◊
-house smoked from NC trout; spreadable

Country Paté ◊
-local pork, rabbit liver; classic course-style with dried cherries

Bologna ◊
-all-beef bologna, lightly grilled

Rabbit Liver Mousse
-local rabbit livers; smooth & mild texture & flavor

Potted Rabbit Rillette ◊
-confit of local rabbit tenderloin; shredded & covered with a thin layer of fat ($3 supplemental charge)

ARTISANAL CHEESE

Four Fat Fowl Creamery 'St. Stephen' with pepitas ◊
-pasteurized cow's milk; triple-cream with buttery & milky overtones with mushroom and grassy notes

Goat Lady Dairy 'Smokey Mountain Round' with arbequina olive oil ◊
-pasteurized goat's milk; light and creamy with a fresh tang

Dutch 5 year Gouda with soba ◊
-pasteurized cow's milk; smooth flavor with a flaky, firm, crystalline texture and a butterscotch finish

Valdeon blue with pear moustarda ◊
-blend of pasteurized cow & goat milk from Spain; dense & inky blue with a smooth, rich and creamy flavor

Deer Creek 'Vat 17' Cheddar with bourbon cherries ◊
-pasteurized cow's milk, firm texture; 2 year aged combination of several cheddars with a sharp and complex flavor

Blue Ridge Creamery 'Jocassee Tomme' with strawberry ◊
-raw cow's milk; crumbly, dense texture; hints of mushroom and grass with a delicate buttery aroma

-We source seasonal products from local & regional farms & artisan producers within the United States. We use sustainable seafood & natural, hormone & antibiotic free meats & proteins.

-No Substitutions please / $10 split plate charge
-20% gratuity may be added to parties of 5 or more

◊ Indicates gluten-free preparation is available.

extra toast points: .50; extra mussel bread: 1.

*Consuming raw or undercooked meats, poultry, seafood, shellfish or eggs may increase your risk of foodborne illness

AMERICAN GROCERY RESTAURANT

Sustainable Seafood Initiative

Fresh on the Menu

American Grocery's menu. *From author's collection.*

Though Chefs David and Susan left the partnership after the first couple years, the Clarkes continued the vision and got great coverage in local and national press. With Darlene's connections in the wine industry and her time spent in California, AGR held regular wine dinner events with industry leaders. Chef Joe was a guest chef at numerous regional events, especially the nationally acclaimed local food, wine and music festival, Euphoria. At these events, the Clarkes preferred to be paired with chefs who shared their philosophy, and opportunities for events with chefs like Katie Button from Asheville and Mike Lata from Charleston were well received by guests. After Thomas Keller met Joe at Euphoria, he returned to Greenville for a team-building trip with his French Laundry staff, and American Grocery was one of the chosen stops.

In 2013, Joe introduced a fun dining experience that was popular in larger dining markets but was new to Greenville. In fact, it was new to South Carolina too. Supper clubs have a long history in the United States, but the newest trend revived in the 2000s. Clarke named his supper club Renegade Vittles and appeared in various mysterious locations that would not be revealed until the day of the event. The invitations went out, chefs were named and a theme was indicated, but the rest was a surprise guaranteed to delight. For the inaugural supper, many of Greenville's top chefs were brought together to collaborate on a five-course meal. Chef Joe Clarke was joined by Michael Kramer from Table301, Jason Scholz from Stella's Southern Bistro, Aaron Manter from the Owl and Anthony Gray from Bacon Brothers, and they each created a course that celebrated the pig for a dinner called Día De Los Puercos. It was a huge success and led to many more unique dining experiences and opportunities for local chefs to work together to build community.

Back at AGR, the beverage program was an important part of the dining experience. The custom wine room held more than 175 handpicked artisan boutique wines drawn from all over the world. Darlene Clarke served as wine director and helped develop the popular seasonal cocktails and spirits. After Kirk Ingram was hired to run the bar in 2013, the cocktail program really took off. The Clarkes began thinking about creating a place that would take well-crafted drinks to the same level of flavor, finish and creativity as they were doing with food at American Grocery. They found the perfect space in 2016 and opened a speakeasy called Vault & Vator. Just as they had pioneered the farm-to-table movement with their restaurant, Vault & Vator pioneered a new genre of beverage experience in Greenville.

As the success of the speakeasy was taking off, several factors came together to threaten the future of American Grocery. In the decade that the restaurant had been open, the explosion of the downtown culinary scene grew to well over one hundred restaurants. Getting quality staff to work the many positions in the front and back of house became a constant problem. Besides having to weather the economic downturn of 2008 and 2009, the owner of the building decided to significantly raise the rent after many years of no rate hike. In July 2017, the Clarkes made the decision to close the restaurant. The news came as a shock to the community, as a place with such a great reputation suddenly had to shut down. In 2020, the Clarkes continue to provide great experiences in Greenville with Vault & Vator and Renegade Vittles.

American Grocery's Honey Glazed Rabbit

4 large rabbit legs
kosher salt to taste
ground black pepper to taste
2 tablespoons canola oil
1 carrot, chopped
1 sweet onion, chopped
½ cup local honey
2 celery ribs, chopped
2 bay leaves
6 sprigs thyme
1 piece ginger, peeled and chopped
4 parsley stems
2 cups chicken stock
1 teaspoon black peppercorns
2 tablespoons white balsamic vinegar

Generously salt and pepper rabbit legs. Preheat oven to 325 degrees. Heat oil in a high-sided braising pan, wait for oil to get hot and quickly brown both sides of the rabbit legs. Remove legs and add onions and carrots to hot oil, being careful not to burn the browned bits left behind by the legs. Once onions have a little color, add remaining ingredients, including browned legs, and bring to a boil. Place lid on pot and put into preheated oven. Braise legs until very tender—begin checking after about an hour. Once legs are fork tender, remove them carefully from the braising liquid and taste liquid for seasoning. Strain solids from liquid, return liquid to stove and reduce to a glaze. It may be necessary to adjust honey or salt levels. The glaze should be syrupy but not thick and not be too salty or too sweet. The acid in the vinegar should help balance the glaze. Glaze legs and serve with the best-quality local vegetables you can find.

3

Bistro Europa

Owners: Andrew and Kelly Baird; Robin Garner and Ben Gold
Years open: 1994–2008
Location: 219 North Main Street

Kelly Bailey lived in Atlanta working as a gourmet foods broker, and her boyfriend Andrew Baird lived in Greenville working as a biochemical engineer at Fluor Daniel. The two would frequently travel between the two cities as they dated and got engaged. In the early 1990s, Atlanta already had a vibrant culinary scene, and many of its restaurants had outdoor seating. This was something Andrew was used to from growing up in England. When Kelly came to Greenville, however, the two couldn't find anywhere in Greenville to enjoy a meal al fresco, nor could they find one that served fresh, Mediterranean-inspired food. Kelly remembers, "I visited many times and loved it. Many things were already in place to make it charming and I could tell it would someday be great."

During their many meals together in Greenville, they noticed that there weren't many options for eating fresh and healthy meals. After years of traveling the world, they wanted to create a place that would bring together ideas they gleaned from places like Europe; Canada; the West Coast; the Southwest; New York City; Washington, D.C.; and England. "If we wanted that kind of food," Kelly reasoned, "then others surely would want it too."

Exterior of Bistro Europa. *Courtesy of Kelly Baird.*

The gears started turning, and in 1993, the couple started planning their next step of opening a restaurant on Main Street. On a drive between College Street and Broad Street in those days, many empty storefronts could be seen. As they began to meet with building owners, they were disappointed to discover that no one would rent to them because their concept didn't match the prevailing attitude of what downtown should be. Kelly recalls that some property owners thought that Main Street should be turned into outlets and were very protective of their properties. Furthermore, rental asking prices were astronomical, so the choices were slim.

Finally, they secured a location at 219 North Main Street, across the street from the Hyatt Regency hotel, one of the most important factors in downtown's revitalization process of the 1980s. The building's owner, former mayor Jim Simpkins, wasn't keen on the décor the couple wanted for their eatery. He preferred a carpeted space with a false ceiling and a metal entryway. Ultimately, something similar to the original façade, with a European feel, was installed. A new aesthetic was brewing, and their restaurant was pioneering it. The interior and storefront were breaking new ground, but Kelly also wanted to add the outdoor seating that they

Interior of Bistro Europa during renovations. *Courtesy of Kelly Baird.*

recognized was missing from the Main Street experience. When Kelly went to city hall to inquire about the matter, everyone she talked to thought that the concept of outdoor seating was crazy.

Demolition of space, which was previously an antique mall, began in January 1994, and the couple worked nonstop for the next eight months, tearing down walls, fixing floors and redoing all surfaces, all while Andrew continued to support them as a full-time engineer with Fluor Daniel. Halfway through the project, a major plumbing issue came up and the whole project was put in jeopardy because they lacked the funds for this unforeseen expense. Carolina First Bank was one of the few local lenders willing to invest in small, local businesses and lent them the money to keep going.

The executive chef was Judy Balsizer, who came from the recently opened 858 Restaurant. Her husband, Bill Balsizer, conveniently worked across the street as executive chef at the Hyatt Regency. She graduated from the Culinary Institute of America and worked in the hotel restaurant industry for years. Judy was right on board with Kelly's desire to bring an array of healthy, fresh and nutritious American entrées with a European and Mediterranean twist. They sought out and acquired produce from local farmers and were at the forefront of the farm-to-table model.

Bistro Europa interior after renovations. *Courtesy of Kelly Baird.*

Next, they had to decide on a name. Kelly wanted it to be called Café Europa, but she later discovered a similar business in Chicago with the same name, so they avoided it because of potential copyright issues. Bistro was a word that was being used more and more in restaurant trends and also communicated a European sensibility, so she settled on it. The doors opened for business in August 1994, but people didn't even have to come in the doors to get a table. Down the street, Rose Marie's Café was the first to apply for sidewalk encroachment approval and put a few tables on the sidewalk earlier that year, but Bistro Europa fully employed an array of sidewalk seating as an integral part of the experience. In 1994, for the first time in Greenville history, outdoor dining on Main Street's sidewalk was an option. Soon, the nearby Village Café, Fuddruckers, Henni's and the Sophisticated Palate followed suit. These pioneering efforts would prove to be one of the distinctive and charming aspects of the modern culinary scene for years to come.

After opening, the owners' commitment to downtown was confirmed by their choice of their wedding reception venue at the Wyche Pavilion along the Reedy River. While that location may seem obvious and fitting in today's terms, in 1995, Kelly and Andrew were the first couple to ever tie the knot in that now-popular wedding venue.

Diners could enjoy Bistro Europa's ambiance seven days a week for breakfast, lunch and dinner at a capacity of seventy guests. For breakfast, guests enjoyed a variety of freshly baked quiches, muffins, croissants, fruit salads and other fresh pick-up selections. Popular lunch items were the eight-inch pizzas, soup of the day, shrimp and sausage fettucine, albacore tuna melt with capers, tuna niçoise salad and a signature herbed chicken salad. Bistro Europa was one of the first places in town to offer large, chef-driven, complex entrée salads all day. Dinner favorites included the pepper-crusted beef tenderloin, tomato baked snapper and herb-roasted double-breasted chicken with cream corn fricassee over garlic mashed potatoes.

Bistro Europa also brought a year-round Sunday brunch to Main Street. Since opening in 1991, Provencia restaurant at the Hyatt Regency across the street had offered Sunday brunches but only on holidays like Easter and other one-time events. Bistro Europa saw the opportunity and attracted crowds every Sunday, serving dishes like smoked frittata with roasted peppers, corn, Mediterranean chicken sausage and cheeses and a smoked salmon eggs benedict. The weekly service was called the Sinatra Brunch, and they played music by Frank Sinatra and Tony Bennett.

Another need they filled and pioneered on Main Street Greenville was as a destination to enjoy an early-morning or a relaxing, after-dinner coffee. Twenty-first-century Greenvillians likely couldn't imagine a time when you couldn't walk downtown with a cup of your favorite coffee from current favorites like Methodical or Port City Java. Until Bistro Europa, though, the sole crafted coffee experiences were at the recently opened Village Café (inside Witterskins bookstore) and the Pony Espresso coffee cart started by Dana Lowie and Steve Taylor (who later started Coffee Underground in 1995), serving weekday mornings and Friday and Saturday evenings. With these three establishments serving on the street and in sidewalk cafés, the downtown Greenville coffee culture was born.

Several key downtown festivals were already in place by the time Bistro Europa opened and contributed to its exposure and success. A weekly music festival, Downtown Alive, had been going on for more than seven years and took place just up Main Street at Piazza Bergamo every Thursday night from spring until fall. The Main Street Jazz Festival on Friday nights began a few years after it opened and kept a steady stream of new customers coming past the door. An annual food event called Fall for Greenville began in 1982, and Bistro Europa immediately began participating as one of thirty-six featured restaurants. Business continued to be heavy every year.

One of the many regular customers was Buck Mickel, one of Greenville's great visionary business leaders, who helped put the plans and investments in place for Greenville's revitalization. Kelly remembers he would come in and always grab the same table in the back of the restaurant and have the biggest smile on his face. She once asked him why he had such a constant grin, and he gladly responded, "I'm so happy about all of great things happening in this city and having a place like your restaurant. Everything that I had visualized has come true."

Andrew Baird continued his engineering job at Fluor Daniel and would help in the evenings and on weekends while Kelly managed the restaurant. Her ambition for Main Street went beyond her bistro doors, though. In 1995, she opened a gift shop called Eden Limited in the restored Cauble Building at the corner of Coffee and Main Streets, though it was originally planned to open in the space next door to the restaurant. In 1999, the Baird's first child was born, and running two downtown establishments proved too difficult. They decided to keep the gift shop and sold Bistro Europa in 2001.

Local restauranteur Robin Garner, co-owner of Garner's Natural Market and Café, had been looking for a downtown location for some time. He partnered with Bistro Europa's executive chef Ben Gold, who had been cooking there since 2000. The new owners built on and expanded the menu options with the addition of vegetarian dishes, continuing the mission to use organic products from local farmers and to recycle. Gold stayed on for several years before leaving in 2003 to travel. He returned to Greenville to spend time working and learning under John Malik at 33 Liberty Restaurant. In 2004, Gold was recharged and took over sole ownership of Bistro Europa.

Gold called his direction "foothills cuisine with a global influence." Popular entrées included pan-roasted duck breast with sweet potato applewood bacon hash and raspberry sauce, shrimp and grits with andouille sausage with cream sauce and salmon with lemon-scallion risotto. The chef/owner sought to balance his family life and ran the restaurant five days a week, closing on Sunday and Monday. In the mid-2000s, there was still decent business, but by then the focus of downtown Greenville's revitalization had transferred to South Main Street, especially in the West End where Falls Park was the centerpiece of the downtown experience. After a great fourteen-year run and playing a key role in the early development of Greenville's culinary scene, Bistro Europa served its last dishes on its sidewalk tables in 2008.

Bistro Europa's Poached Pears

1 ½ cups Cabernet Sauvignon
2 cups port wine
2 cups sugar
3 sprigs thyme
2 bay leaves
12 whole white peppercorns
3 parsley stems
5 cups water
2 vanilla beans, split and seeded
1 juniper berry
12 pears
1 pound crumbled Roquefort cheese
herb mix
salt and pepper to taste

Place all ingredients except pears in a pot and bring to a boil. Reduce to a simmer. Peel and core the pears and add them to the pot. Cover with parchment paper. Take off heat and allow to steep for twenty to thirty minutes. Place pears in a casserole dish, pour liquid over them and chill in a refrigerator overnight. Add one tablespoon of herb mix (chive, tarragon, chervil and basil) to one pound of crumbled Roquefort cheese. When pears are cool, stuff with cheese and herb mix. For the sauce, strain poaching liquid. Bring to a boil and add two tablespoons cornstarch diluted with four tablespoons of water to poaching liquid. Simmer for five minutes. Season with salt and pepper. Pour over pears.

4
Devereaux's

Owners: Steven Devereaux Greene, Ed Greene, Justin Tilley, Daniel Greene
  and Spencer Thomson; Carl Sobocinski and Stewart Spinks
Years open: 2005–2012
Location: 25 East Court Street

Working in a kitchen is something Steven Devereaux Greene was used to for most of life. First learning from his mother in the small town of Ninety-Six, South Carolina, then getting his first cooking job at fifteen working under Chef Pascal Hurtebize in Greenwood, he soon started on a trajectory that would land him his first restaurant ownership at just twenty-five years old. To get there, he moved to the best culinary destination in South Carolina (and perhaps the Southeast), Charleston. He first worked at 82 Queen Restaurant and then under Chef Michael Kramer at McCrady's. This firm foundation in fine dining, classic food techniques and contemporary plating, as well as service that matched the highest standards of food preparation, landed the young chef a key position as chef de cuisine of the Mobile five-star Woodland's Resort and Inn in Summerville, South Carolina. The restaurant was led by Executive Chef Ken Vedrinski, who earned the destination the only five-star rating in the state. Chef Greene gleaned even more knowledge here from the haute cuisine style taught by Vedrinksi. Steven's friend Chef Spencer Thomson had also worked with him at all three of these restaurants.

Exterior view of the 1903 building where Devereaux's occupied the first floor. *From author's collection.*

In 2005, Chef Greene pursued his dream of opening a restaurant in Greenville, South Carolina, and partnered with his two brothers and uncle to open Devereaux's in the heart of this up-and-coming food city. His brother Edward Greene was the general manager, and his other brother, Justin Tilley, was the restaurant manager and wine director, while his uncle Daniel Greene was the executive managing partner. Soon, the restaurant would set a new bar for cuisine in Greenville.

Greene used the idea of the charm of old brick buildings like at McCrady's in Charleston and found a space on the floor of a 1903 cigar factory (which ironically moved to Charleston in 1930). Though two other restaurants prior to Devereaux's failed in that location, this confident team was not daunted. They knew they were bringing a level of food and service that this city hadn't been exposed to yet. The décor was modern yet cozy, it sat 150 guests and had a large open kitchen window and a chef's "pass" table where dishes would receive their final touches before being served. Service was never rushed, and the highly trained staff was ready to explain cooking techniques, wine tasting notes or any other help that would make the experience special. When food was served to more than two people, extra staff would come to help deliver the dishes in a choreographed, simultaneous lowering of the plates in front of the guests.

The concept was contemporary American cuisine with a fusion ranging from the West Coast to the Lowcountry to French, Italian and Asian styles.

Interior view of Devereaux's private dining room, showing the choreographed setting of plates during an At the Chef's Table Culinary Tour. *From author's collection.*

An early signature appetizer was the hoisin-glazed quail breast with lychee nuts and candied turnips. A signature entrée was an Asian-spiced rack of Colorado lamb with Nishiki rice risotto, baby carrots and lemongrass. One of the unique and delicious bar menu items was the house-made truffle tater tots. Soups in most restaurants are brought out in full bowls from the kitchen. Not here. The liquid cools off too much and it sloshes up onto the sides of the bowl, so Devereaux's served soup with the garnish chopped up into a cone shape in the middle of an empty soup bowl, and the piping hot soup was poured into the garnished bowl tableside.

One of the things that really set Devereaux's apart was the tasting menu. Nowhere else in Greenville was this kind of specialty menu offered on a daily basis. Guests could choose between a preset five-course chef's tasting menu for $75 or the "ultimate" tasting menu that comprised ten spontaneous courses of the chef's choosing, all for $120 per person.

One example of a ten-course "ultimate" menu included:

- An amuse bouche consisting of crab salad with cumin and carrot puree
- Tasmanian salmon sashimi served with cucumber flower
- A two-part dish with apple and beet tartar and a gazpacho soup with beef
- Celery root soup with smoked bacon and potato

- Grilled tiger prawn with apple salad
- Foie gras on a French baguette with bittersweet chocolate and passion fruit
- Japanese red snapper in bonito broth
- Quail prepared three ways: flash-fried quail leg encrusted with panko and stuffed with beef tenderloin, pan seared quail breast and quail risotto
- Sous vide beef short rib over Anson Mills grits with glaze
- Roquefort cheese and jam
- Lemon posset (pre-dessert palate cleanser)
- Carrot cake with vanilla ice cream

The ensuing years brought some great accolades, exposure and experiences for Chef Greene. In January 2007, Chef Greene and Executive Sous Chef Spencer Thomson were invited to cook at the James Beard House in New York. Greene remembers a dining experience at Jean-Georges in New York as being monumental in his career, saying, "Here this young chef from some small town in South Carolina visits, and Jean-Georges himself comes out to greet us and treated us like we were something special. I learned a lot about hospitality that day."

Two years later, Guy Savoy (a famous three-starred Michelin chef from Paris) and Thomas Keller (America's biggest "rock star" chef) of the French Laundry cooked at Devereaux's. Chef Thomson went on to do a one-month stage at Guy Savoy's restaurant in Paris. Greene recalls Chef Keller calling him "Chef" when he was in the Devereaux's kitchen and trusting the staff to make important decisions about the special dinner being served—another great occasion for growth and learning. Keller was so impressed with Chef Greene that he invited him to stage for one month at French Laundry in Napa Valley. Greene remembers "learning how to run a restaurant like a well-oiled machine."

In February 2007, Court Square Dining Group owner Carl Sobocinski and convenience store/gas station chain owner Stewart Spinks bought the controlling interest in a new Devereaux's partnership that included Executive Chef Steven Greene, Executive Sous Chef Spencer Thomson and Wine Director Justin Tilley.

Chef Greene decided to continue pushing himself to new levels and moved on from his namesake restaurant to become the chef de cuisine at the five-star Umstead Hotel and Spa in Cary, North Carolina, in 2009. By then, Spencer Thomson was more than ready for his own advancement and moved into the executive chef position at Devereaux's. A year later, Greenville History Tours' owner, and author, John Nolan partnered with Table301 to start the first culinary tour in town, called At the Chef's Table Culinary Tour. Devereaux's was one of the five featured restaurants and gave locals and tourists a biweekly opportunity to sample its impeccable flavors and service.

When Chef Spencer Thomson told guests about the dish, which was different every time, he loved to share how he exclusively used Anson Mills grits from Columbia. The founder, Glenn Roberts, resurrected a Carolina heirloom corn-grain called John Haulk yellow dent corn. Through research, growing and harvesting the corn, and through trial and error, Roberts rediscovered the cold milling process that brought out the best flavor for the processed grits.

Chef Thomson was also at the helm when George Clooney was in town for a few months filming *Leatherheads* at the nearby Westin Poinsett Hotel. Devereaux's soon became a favorite for Clooney. In his first few visits, not very many people noticed him there. Social media (then in its infancy) got word around that he was eating there, and soon paparazzi outside made leaving the restaurant difficult. Thomson told Clooney that he could slip out the back door of the kitchen. Once out, he hopped a few fences and made it back to the hotel without a big delay.

Another story Thomson recalled involved the wall of large arched mirrors that lined one side of the dining room. While the mirrors made the space look much larger, they also look like passageways. People frequently ran into the mirrors, and the staff in the kitchen jokingly called them "window walkers." On New Year's Eve, a friend of Thomson's was a bit tipsy and went across the room to use the restroom. He proceeded to walk into the mirror. He politely excused himself to the person in the mirror. He tried again, bumped the mirror and excused himself again. Thomson finally noticed him and told him to go around the other way.

For many people, Devereaux's was a place to go for a special occasion and to get a fine dining experience that was certainly not ordinary. Though it was an expensive restaurant, regulars found themselves there several times a week. The Dovers, Dickersons, Browns and Bannisters were some of these familiar faces who not only were great patrons but also became good friends with the staff, owners and chefs.

By 2013, a combination of factors, including continued effects of the recession and lease issues with the building owner, precipitated the closing of this pioneering restaurant. Chef Greene returned to Greenville to be

Above: Example of a dish served on the At the Chef's Table Culinary Tour. *From author's collection.*

Left: Jeff and Olga Bannister were some of the regulars of Devereaux's—often dining there three to five times a week. *Courtesy of Jeff Bannister.*

featured in a series of special guest dinners that also included Chef Scott Crawford of the Umstead Hotel and Spa and a Devereaux's reunion dinner involving all the primary staff who contributed to its success over the years.

Devereux's Heirloom Squash Soup

Squash Soup
8–10 heirloom squash
1 yellow onion
3 leeks (white only)
3 shallots
5 garlic cloves
¼ pound unsalted butter
½ quart heavy cream

Cut squash, onion and leeks into ½ inch pieces. Thinly slice shallot and garlic. Sweat the onion, leeks, shallot and garlic until translucent in butter. Add squash and cover. Leave on very low heat for ten minutes. Squash should have released water content. Add heavy cream and bring to a boil. Once liquid boils pull pot off the stove and blend in a Vita-Prep and pass thru a chinois. Season with salt to taste.

Tater Tot
2 Idaho potatoes
1 egg white
2 tablespoons chopped truffle
black truffle oil to taste
salt to taste

Wash potatoes and then wrap in aluminum foil. Roast at 400 degrees for forty minutes. The potatoes should not be cooked fully. Cool potatoes in the refrigerator and then peel. Shred through the large side of a box grater. Wearing gloves and using your hands, add egg white and chopped truffle. Add truffle oil and salt to taste. Either deep fry the tots for three minutes at 400 degrees or pan fry in clarified butter until all sides are golden brown.

Melted Onion
2 Vidalia onions
2 tablespoons water
¼ pound butter
1 tablespoon chopped fresh chive

Julienne onions, place into a two-quart sauce pot. Add water and butter and cover. Cook until very tender and translucent. Slice chive and add to the pot. Season to taste. To serve, place a tablespoon of the melted onions in the center of the plate. Stack two or three tater tots on top of the onions. Pour the hot soup around the onion and tater tots and enjoy.

5

High Cotton Maverick Bar and Grill

Owner: Richard Elliott
Years open: 2007–2015
Location: 550 South Main Street

The Maverick Southern Kitchens Group was one of the most revered restaurant groups in Charleston—an enviable position in a city that is now considered one of the great culinary destinations not only in the South but also in the country. Richard Elliott, owner of the group, built an impressive array of Charleston properties, including Slightly North of Broad (SNOB) in 1993 with Frank Lee as executive chef, High Cotton Maverick Bar & Kitchen in 1999 and the Old Village Post House in 2003, along with a popular cookware retail shop, Charleston Cooks!. As Greenville's culinary scene grew in diversity, size and regional and national fame, Charleston restauranteurs began to take notice. In 2004, a Mount Pleasant barbecue chain, Sticky Fingers, came to Greenville's Main Street.

In 2007, when Richard Elliott decided to bring the group's first restaurant expansion outside of Charleston to Greenville, the city's culinary landscape took a major step forward. Tbonz Restaurant Group followed, bringing Liberty Tap Room & Grill to Main Street next to the newly opened West End Field baseball stadium (now Fluor Field at the West End).

High Cotton's reputation for finely crafted southern and American dishes served with high-end ambiance and hospitality came to Greenville.

"High cotton" is an old southern term for living well when high-growing cotton on a plantation was a sign of prosperity. That feeling of prosperity was present in this new location. Situated in the newly built Riverplace development, the views of the Reedy River outside the three-story dining room's walls of glass were the best in town. Fine tablecloths covered each table and impeccably set tableware was accompanied by leather-bound menus. While the old-world, brick-walled charm of Charleston's High Cotton couldn't translate to the new space, the elegance was equally effective in Greenville's modern building. Dining was spread across three levels, with several private dining rooms for more intimate functions. To help ease the transition of cuisine, Executive Chef Jason Scholz and Chef Jason Hackett moved to Greenville after years of running the kitchen in Charleston.

The menu's American fare was filled with meats, game, fresh fish and organic produce sourced as locally as possible. For starters, the baby spinach salad came with pulled duck confit, dried cranberries, hard cooked duck egg and warm andouille vinaigrette. The strawberry and golden beet salad was served over arugula and hazelnut goat cheese croquette with champagne-herb vinaigrette. A seafood example was the Carolina Blue Crab Cake with

High Cotton (*left*) was one of the opening restaurants in the Riverplace complex and had an incredible view of the Riverwalk. *From author's collection.*

asparagus, forest mushrooms, preserved lemon and piquillo pepper aioli. Fresh fowl came by way of a bacon-wrapped quail with quinoa, medjool dates, spiced pecans, whole-grain mustard BBQ and apple slaw.

Steak options included a twelve-ounce angus rib-eye, eleven-ounce New York strip and a seven-ounce filet mignon. Examples of the seasonal entrées include the sweet potato and eggplant lasagna with house-made tomato sauce, arugula and warm vinaigrette; Carolina Grouper with Lowcountry red rice, rock shrimp, citrus emulsion and shaved fennel salad; Maverick Shrimp and Grits with stone-ground yellow corn grits, country ham, andouille sausage and a tomato scallion pan sauce; Sunburst Farms Trout with fingerling potatoes, cauliflower, forest mushrooms and marcona almond romesco; apple-mustard glazed pork chop with brown sugar baked Sea Island red peas, charred broccolini and bacon-bourbon jus; and the Cervena venison with pancetta-roasted brussels sprouts, butternut squash puree and blackberry madeira reduction.

High Cotton's opening coincided with the filming of George Clooney's film *Leatherheads*, and the restaurant became the star-gazing spot for local fans to get a glimpse of actress Renee Zellweger. With this celebrity boost adding to the already strong local buzz, Greenville's High Cotton revenues almost matched that of its sister Charleston location. When the owners opened in 2007, they did not know that a major recession would hit the country within a year. Expensive restaurants in Greenville all felt the hit. Some, like Devereaux's, Stax's Peppermill and High Cotton were able to remain viable. Others, like 33 Liberty and Restaurant O could not weather the economic downturn.

One of High Cotton's responses to the situation was to advertise a new happy hour menu to attract budget-conscious patrons. Besides well-priced crafted cocktails, guests could get a premium beef burger with hand-cut fries for just five dollars. A serving of six scratch-made barbecue ribs with cabbage and carrot coleslaw could also be enjoyed for five dollars. For a dollar less, a serving of tempura-battered portabella fries came with a side of béarnaise dipping sauce.

During the recession, Executive Chef Jason Scholz left the restaurant to open up his own, Stella's Southern Bistro, in the suburb of Simpsonville. Sous Chef Jason Hackett was promoted to chef du cuisine, while Anthony Gray became executive chef of both the Charleston and Greenville locations. Menus changed over the years, and the frequency of chef changes caused some guests to sense a disruption in the consistency of the experience, though the chefs were all well trained and accomplished.

A view of the lower dining room of High Cotton. A few of the dining guests are Ken Talbott and Paul Barnard. *From author's collection.*

Gregory McPhee led the kitchen as executive chef for almost a year in 2012 and 2013 and was replaced by Chef Adrian Carpenter for the restaurant's remaining years.

In the transition between the last two chefs, Greenville History Tours partnered with High Cotton and several other southern food restaurants to create an immersive experience for locals and visitors to sample iconic southern dishes. The tour was called Tastes of the South and featured fried green tomatoes at Soby's New South Cuisine; shrimp and grits at High Cotton; chicken gumbo soup and fried gator bites at Ford's Oyster House & Cajun Kitchen; barbecue pork, brisket and collards at Smoke on the Water; and a pecan tart with bourbon ice cream at Breakwater Restaurant. The tour was a great success, bringing locals into High Cotton who thought it might to too "high cotton" for them, and received notice in articles in the *Atlanta Journal Constitution*, *Charleston Post and Courier*, *Ebony* magazine and *Garden & Gun* magazine.

In 2016, Richard Elliott announced that he was getting out of the restaurant business to pursue family obligations and run for mayor of Charleston. Hall Management Group acquired all of the restaurants and cookware stores and made significant changes. Following customer consensus, Bill Hall, owner of the group, brought his nationally recognized Charleston steakhouse Hall's Chophouse to take over the High Cotton restaurant space in January 2016. Charleston's High Cotton location continued to remain in business.

High Cotton's Ricotta Gnocchi

6 ounces unsalted butter
1 ½ cups water
2 cups all-purpose flour
salt (to taste)
2 tablespoons Dijon mustard
1 tablespoon chopped chives
1 tablespoon chopped tarragon
1 tablespoon chopped mint
1 cup goat milk ricotta cheese

Melt the butter in a heavy-bottom pot, add water and flour. Stir with a wooden spoon over medium-high heat. Season the mixture with salt and continue to stir until dough becomes very smooth and pulls away from the sides. Remove dough from heat and transfer to a small tabletop mixer fitted with a paddle attachment. Add mustard, herbs and cheese and slowly beat until well mixed. Once incorporated, add in eggs one at a time, mixing thoroughly after each addition. Place dough in a pastry bag and let it rest for forty-five minutes. Meanwhile, bring a large pot of water to a boil and season with salt. Once rested, slowly squeeze the dough out of the pastry bag, cutting ½-inch pieces with scissors directly into boiling water. The gnocchi are done when they begin to float. Remove gnocchi from water and let them rest on a plate lined with parchment paper. Allow to dry and then sauté in butter and add your favorite vegetables.

6

Neue Southern Food Truck

Owners: Lauren Zanardelli and Graham Foster
Years open: 2012–14
Location: Various locations, primarily at "Stone's Point" on Wade
   Hampton Boulevard

In 2010, after starting in nonculinary careers, Lauren Zanardelli (an elementary school teacher) and Graham Foster (a personal trainer and cyclist) both enrolled at the Johnson & Wales Culinary School in Charlotte, North Carolina, to pursue their cooking passions. The couple met serendipitously in the school's Stocks, Sauces and Soups course and began to date while sweating over the process of making the perfect bone broth.

After graduating, they embarked on a European travel adventure to taste the flavors of the world in the countries of their origin and witness authentic cooking processes and plating firsthand. Internships at Michelin-star restaurants (Public, Saxon & Parole and Wallse) in New York City brought them back to the United States before coming to Greenville, South Carolina, with the ambition of pioneering the food truck scene here. By then, the national food truck craze was in full swing. Two years before they started this venture in Foster's hometown, another Greenville native, Tyler Florence, began hosting the wildly popular Food Network show the *Great Food Truck Race*. This survivor-style reality show combined the drama of ordinary people competing against each other with the food truck trend that was sweeping the country in the wake of the economic downturn of the early 2000s.

Years of frugal saving and months of planning an exciting menu helped prepare them for this exciting new path. Unfortunately, Greenville was not prepared for food trucks. Outdated city zoning laws limited their opportunities to become part of the fabric of the downtown culinary scene, with stipulations like no parking in public spaces, requirement of having a bathroom nearby and needing to prepare food in a permanent commercial kitchen. Even if they wanted to park outside of city boundaries, a thirty-minute maximum time limit in public spaces negated any real attempt at selling food or making a profit. The solution for early food trucks was to park outside city limits in private parking lots with agreement from the owners.

Despite these significant hurdles, the truck developed a cult-like following among the millennial and foodie crowd, who were baited on each Facebook (4,200 followers at peak) or Twitter (2,200 followers at peak) post about where they would be serving and what the daily features were. The name Neue Southern was decided for the food truck. *Neue* is pronounced "noy-ah" and it means "new" in German. On the truck, it was wrapped in a bright orange color with dark red writing and graphics and stood out wherever it drove or parked.

The new southern fare was meant to feature European cuisine inspired by local southern ingredients. After a research trip to Asian countries in 2013, inspiration from Vietnam, Japan, Saigon and Hong Kong cuisines were also infused. The daily changing menu items had elements of Asian, European and a variety of American flavor profiles. One of the early favorites was the schnitzel sandwich made of Heritage Farms pork loin, house-made pickle, local tomato, slaw and lemon cream on a buttered Bavarian Pretzel Factory's hard roll. My personal favorite was the Banh-Mi sandwich and the Tonkotsu ramen soup. Other dishes found on the menu at various times were the pork belly steamed bun, falafel, Okonomiyaki potatoes and BBQ pomme frites. However, the hands-down favorite menu item that brought many patrons back daily was the brussels sprouts.

After almost two years of triumphs and setbacks, Zanardelli and Foster made the hard but exciting decision to leave Greenville and head west to the Mecca of the food truck and food cart scene in Portland, Oregon. Zanardelli wrote an emotional note to the masses of faithful followers, saying,

We know this comes as a huge surprise. It's all happened extremely quickly. What seemed like some vague, distant idea became a reality overnight and

Above: Chef Lauren Zanardelli cooking inside the food truck. *From author's collection.*

Left: Menu for Neue Southern. *From author's collection.*

we're still in a state of shock ourselves! Graham and I knew when we started our business that our future would always be a little unpredictable. From the time we opened until now, we've been asked what our next step will be, and that question, at best, has been met by us with shrugs. We've known that in a few years' time we want to be working toward opening our brick-and-mortar restaurant. But until recently, we didn't know what the years in between would hold. We spent the last six months exploring every possible direction. What can I say? We've both dreamed about one day living on the west coast. And we're so fortunate to have this opportunity to spend a few years in a progressive culinary city. We'll be learning and absorbing everything we can before we move back east to kill it in OUR restaurant. We feel like we need to take it.

Zanardelli and Foster set up shop with their new food cart in the Gantry in Portland and continued to gain a faithful following and garner further inspiration from fellow chefs. In 2018, after several years of success, they moved to Mount Lebanon, Pennsylvania, near Zanardelli's hometown of Pittsburgh to finally achieve the goal of opening their own brick-and-mortar restaurant. At the Fairlane the couple have applied all of their years of experiences into creating a restaurant that promises to occupy their creative culinary talents for many years to come.

The food truck scene has become extensive since the pioneering days of Neue Southern. Though the city's zoning laws are still prohibitive of a meaningful downtown presence, more than thirty food trucks of all types and flavors now serve the growing Greenville foodie crowd. For those who were here when it all started, Neue Southern will always have a place in their hearts. And, oh, those brussels sprouts.

Neue Southern Brussels Sprouts Recipe

3 cups apple cider vinegar
1 ⅔ cups white granulated sugar
1 pinch red chile flakes for desired heat level
canola oil for frying
cleaned, trimmed, halved brussels sprouts
salt

Combine vinegar, sugar and chile flakes into pot. Bring to a boil and continue to cook on medium high heat until reduced by nearly half. Cool completely. Using a deep fryer or deep sided Dutch oven, bring oil to 350 degrees. Fry brussels sprouts in small batches until deep brown. A spatter guard will come in handy. Drain completely of excess oil and place in a large bowl. Salt to taste and add desired amount of cooled gastrique. A little goes a long way. Toss until brussels are evenly coated.

7

Nippon Center Yagoto

Owners: Kiyohiro and Chigusa Tsuzuki
Years open: 1990–2001
Location: 500 Congaree Road

Kiyohiro Tsuzuki came to the United States from Japan in the late 1960s and was one of the pioneers of Japanese investment in the United States. His company, TNS Inc., began as a textile corporation but later diversified into the restaurant business by first buying Anthony's in Atlanta. Next came the Seven Oaks restaurant in Greenville and then the Nippon Center Yagoto as the first to reflect Tsuzuki's native culture. His company joined the growing ranks of Japanese companies located in Greenville, including the firms of Fuji, Hitachi, Mita and Nicca, which came here in the 1980s.

Though Kiyohiro's company was the financial powerhouse behind the restaurant, his wife, Chigusa, was the driving force behind its creation. The couple had a strong desire to give back to their adopted hometown of Greenville and thought that sharing authentic aspects of their Japanese culture would be a special contribution. While most restauranteurs focus on the business aspects of their enterprises, Chigusa sought to create a spiritual experience of the Japanese culture through immersive exposure to its food, sense of home, architecture and a traditional Japanese garden.

For the architecture, chief architect K. Taniguchi incorporated woods imported from Japan, including cypress, cedar, cherry, elm, Douglas fir and bamboo, which were left in their natural state to show off the neutral colors

Exterior view of the Nippon Center Yagoto complex. *Courtesy of Yuri Tsuzuki.*

and textures. Japanese carpenters were also brought in to create a space in which every room had access and views to the central rock garden. Freshly cut flowers arranged in the Japanese style delighted the senses of sight and smell. Guests were encouraged to remove their shoes for dining but could opt for a "Western style" seating if needed. The various dining rooms reflected Japanese cuisine from different regions and historical periods, appointed with black-lacquer furniture—some examples were hundreds of years old. The main dining room featured cuisines from the sixteenth, seventeenth and eighteenth centuries, as well as modern selections. One dining room specialized in serving tempura dishes while another featured teppanyaki in addition to a dedicated space for a sushi bar. Perhaps the most popular main dish was the shabu-shabu—a choice that had a wow factor in which a pot of boiling water was brought to the guests and meat and vegetables were added and cooked in front of them.

To further the Japanese experience for guests, authentic tea ceremonies (or *sado*) took place in a special *chanoyu* room. The first room of this kind in the United States was found in the Japanese embassy in Washington, D.C., and Greenville's was the second.

One of the dining rooms of the Nippon Center Yagoto. The sunken chairs accommodated those who preferred to sit in the traditional American style. *Courtesy of Yuri Tsuzuki.*

A traditional Japanese tea ceremony demonstration. *Courtesy of Yuri Tsuzuki.*

The Tsuzukis and their restaurant were soon followed by another significant Japanese investment ($150 million) in Greenville, when Hitachi built a plant in 1991 to manufacture television picture tubes. Opening celebrations, of course, took place at the Nippon Center. The center continued to be an incentive for further Japanese investment when a stadium seating firm called GDS Seating Inc. located here in 1995.

Over the years, guests could attend culturally enriching events like ice sculpture displays, multiweek cooking courses led by Chef Tshiaki Suzuki and Executive Chef Hisamichi "Fuji" Fujimura. The daily menu consisted of dishes emphasizing fresh and natural ingredients. Plating was an important component of the experience, with the food artistically arranged and presented on plain pottery or other natural materials like wood or rock.

To the great sorrow of locals, the restaurant closed in early 2001, with the hopes that the fifteenth century–style building and its gardens would be preserved with adaptive educational and functional use. After years of unfulfilled plans and neglect, the once-beautiful building was torn down in 2016.

The legacy of the Tsuzuki family continues in the city in significant ways. Chigura's love of dogwood trees led her to donate scores of them to be planted in the downtown and public areas, and their beauty still enhances the city today. The family's $1 million donation for the building of the Peace Center for the Performing Arts was a significant part of making that world-class cultural amenity a reality. Furthermore, the family funded one of city's most scenic and serene places to visit, the Place of Peace at Furman University. It is a traditional Japanese temple brought from the Tsuzukis' family land in Japan, disassembled into 2,400 pieces and reassembled in 2008 by Japanese artisans near Furman's iconic lake. Though the Yagoto restaurant is now gone, this authentic Japanese cultural space will continue to inspire and enhance our community for generations to come.

8

Restaurant O

Owners: Carl Sobocinski, David Williams, Rodney Freidank and Lee Lawson
Years open: 2003–2008
Location: 116 South Main Street

When Restaurant O opened in 2003, owners Carl Sobocinski and David Williams had six years of sustained success under their belts from their first restaurant, Soby's New South Cuisine. Long-term planning involved expanding with diversified restaurants within the downtown Greenville core, so when the Poinsett Hotel renovation was announced in the late 1990s, the pair knew this would be the next step.

The historic Poinsett Hotel was built in 1925 and was a monument of grandeur from Greenville's textile past. However, beginning in the late 1980s, the building sat vacant for thirteen years, with homeless people taking up residence beyond its boarded-up doors. A strong consideration was given to tear it down, but some Charleston investors decided to bring it back to life with a $25 million renovation and open it as the Westin Poinsett Hotel.

To the right of the restaurant space, the new Carolina First Bank office building with the Poinsett Plaza at its entrance was another $25 million investment.

Sobocinski and Williams signed the lease for their new space between the two major projects in 2000 and added another $2 million investment of their own. Upscale clients were readily available from the nearby Peace Center

Exterior view of Restaurant O. *Courtesy of the Table301 Restaurant Group.*

performances, bank executives and traveling corporate leaders staying at the five-star hotel. In 2001, shortly after leasing this space, they deepened their commitment to downtown by opening a bakery/deli called Soby's on the Side at 22 East Court Street, with a corporate apartment/private dining space above it called the Loft at Soby's.

Restaurant O took its name from the distinctive typeface of the Soby's restaurant logo across the street. Its simplicity and ambiguity reflect the trends in America's most important culinary markets like Las Vegas, Chicago and New York City. Beyond the name, the style of décor and presentation of food brought an authentic big-city atmosphere that was a completely new experience for locals. It was sleek and cosmopolitan, with accents of metal and glass. Near the entrance was a nine-foot waterfall that provided tranquility and soft sounds of running water. Stairs near the entrance led up to a mezzanine O Lounge that overlooked part of the first floor as well as Greenville's Main Street. A brushed chrome bar, lounge seating with sleek couches and leather chairs and private booths—complete with curtains ready to be drawn—made the upstairs space distinctive. The first-floor main dining room accommodated one hundred guests with custom seating—like the circular table in the front corner that perfectly echoed the curved corner wall. Additional seating options included a beautifully appointed private dining room that housed the wine cellar and outdoor dining along the front and sides of the building. Behind the scenes, Executive Chef Rodney Freidank had two state-of-the-art kitchens at his staff's disposal—a main kitchen with a special steak broiler capable of 1,650-degree temperatures and a separate prep kitchen.

The cosmopolitan restaurant opened with a Hollywood-like premiere. While there was no movie, there were Hollywood stars. The BMW Celebrity Pro-Am Golf Tournament was being held during the same week the restaurant launched. A red carpet walk of fame was held at the Westin Poinsett Hotel next door (where many of the guests were staying), including the likes of Kevin Costner, Cheech Marin, Steve Gatlin, Steve Bartkowski, Tommy Lasorda, Michael O'Keefe, Gabrielle Reece and Darius Rucker. The celebrities walked from the hotel to Restaurant O for an evening cocktail party. The city was star-struck and turned out in droves to get a glimpse of the stars. It was a night to remember not only for the restaurant staff but for all of Greenville. This celebrity-studded beginning led to Restaurant O being the place to go for future well-known visitors like George Clooney, Renee Zellweger, Natalie Cole, Tom Brokaw, John McCain, Rudy Giuliani and John Kerry.

The menu featured classic steaks and chops similar to a classic chophouse, but the bulk of the menu was reserved for a rotating selection of eclectic entrées driven by fresh, local ingredients. Some local farmers were even hired to grow items exclusively for Restaurant O.

For starters, selections from the daily changing menu included confit of Muscovy duck legs with arugula, fennel, pink grapefruit and bigarade sauce; pecan smoked trout salad with smoked Atlantic salmon, crayfish relish, truffle oil, capers and red onion; and cold water oysters on the half shell with traditional cocktail sauce. the creamy blue crab and Vidalia onion soup became one of the most popular signature dishes.

Steaks were the specialty and featured USDA choice beef with a twenty-four-ounce porterhouse, sixteen-ounce New York Strip, seven-ounce filet mignon and a sixteen-ounce rib-eye as the primary selections. The eight-ounce Snake River Farms American "Kobe" flat iron steak was something found nowhere else in the area. Some nonsteak options fired up in the 1,650-degree oven were the Bell and Evans natural chicken breast and the twelve-ounce main lobster tail. The lobster could also be ordered as surf and turf, either broiled or batter-fried.

One of the elegant specialty booth seats in Restaurant O's main dining room. *Courtesy of the Table301 Restaurant Group.*

A sweet finish included choices like the Tahitian vanilla bean crème brûlée with hazelnut butter cookie; the Callebaut chocolate bombe with milk chocolate marquis, coconut-white chocolate center and sour cream compote; the deconstructed banana split; and the warm blueberry pound cake with coconut ice cream, macadamia praline and white chocolate.

View of Restaurant O's dining room. *Courtesy of the Table301 Restaurant Group.*

Restaurant O was quite a sensation in Greenville's maturing culinary scene. It was certainly the place to go to commemorate a special occasion like an anniversary, birthday, promotion or wedding. However, local perception was that it was only for that—special occasions. The higher price point, impeccable atmosphere and dress code dissuaded some from thinking of Restaurant O for a regular evening out. In 2006, management responded with changes, including efforts to communicate a more welcoming message, switching to a smoke free environment, abolishing the dress code and implementing an affordable thirty-five-dollar pre-fixe menu of three courses.

Community outreach efforts took a large step forward that year, and Sobocinski partnered with local musician Edwin McCain to create a new annual food, wine and music festival called Southern Exposure. Top chefs, great bands and notable wine makers created unique experiences, and proceeds supported local nonprofit charities. It was a huge success that went on to become the most anticipated food events of the year (later renamed Euphoria), attracting nationally renowned chefs and food writers. Greenville was appearing on America's culinary map.

In 2008, the economic recession proved too difficult for the restaurant to continue. A 12 percent drop in sales from the previous year was the writing

A creative tuna appetizer from Restaurant O's menu. *Courtesy of the Table301 Restaurant Group.*

on the wall that a rough road was ahead if it proceeded. Another factor affecting the decision involved the 2007 acquisition of the former high-end competitor Devereaux's. Trying to maintain two high–price point restaurants through a recession didn't make economic sense. In Restaurant O's final months, Carl Sobocinski made an unprecedented show of gratitude to the community by offering pay what you wish events that let both regulars and newcomers enjoy one of the best meals in the city for a price that they could afford. It was the kind of gesture that reinforced and sealed people's loyalty to the restaurant group—one that in 2020 remains the largest and most revered in the city.

Rodney's Split Creek Farms' Feta Cheese and Watermelon Salad

1–2 pounds seedless red watermelon (rind removed)
1–2 pounds seedless gold watermelon (rind removed)
4 handfuls organic field greens
kosher salt and black pepper, to taste
4 tablespoons infused balsamic reduction (see below)
2 tablespoons pistachio oil
4 ounces Split Creek feta in brine (drained and crumbled)
curried pistachios (optional)

Slice watermelon thin by hand or on a mandolin. Cut slices into circles using a biscuit cutter. Shingle watermelon across plate, alternating colors, using eight slices total per portion. Toss field greens with salt, pepper, some balsamic reduction and some pistachio oil. Drizzle plate and melon with remaining balsamic reduction and pistachio oil. Crumble feta onto greens and watermelon and garnish with pistachios if desired.

Rodney's Infused Balsamic Reduction

1 32-ounces bottle balsamic vinegar
¼ cup sugar
1 teaspoon molasses
1 teaspoon Worcestershire sauce
1 piece star anise

2 tablespoons honey
¼ cup dry currants
¼ cup dry cranberries
2 black peppercorns
1 vanilla bean
1 sprig rosemary

Combine all ingredients in a saucepan and reduce slowly until syrupy consistency.

9
The 858

Owners: Carl Sobocinski, Todd King and Larry Grosshans; Kip Wynne,
   John Kirk and Steve Boone
Years open: 1993–98
Location: 18 East North Street

It may not be surprising that perhaps the most progressive restaurant in the early stages of Greenville's modern culinary scene was started by ambitious young men fresh out of college. Todd King and Carl Sobocinski graduated from Clemson University and were familiar with the strides the city was making in its downtown revitalization. King purchased the four-story Devore office building on East North Street when he was just twenty-four years old.

It was near the most vibrant section of town at the time, the block of North Main between North and College, where the Hyatt Regency was located. The Devore's décor was art deco and it took significant investment to get it functioning as a restaurant. It also included a five-thousand-square-foot banquet hall, condominium, office and retail space. The restaurant's second-floor location meant that guests would enter at the ground floor in a tasteful foyer where the original art deco elevator would take them up to the second floor. The restaurant dining space was then dramatically revealed when the doors opened. As for the name, the pair derived it from the historic use of the space as the former

Lodge No. 858 from the Benevolent Protective Order of the Elks organization that occupied it for forty years.

Atlanta had the most advanced culinary scene in the Southeast at the time, and the 858 was able to lure Larry Grosshans away from Atlanta's Buckhead Diner to be head chef. The restaurant opened on November 19, 1993, with seating for 110 people and a staff of 30 to serve lunch and dinner. The kitchen did not need a lot of additional work, as it was previously an industrial kitchen that was used for the frequent Elks Lodge banquets. Word quickly spread about the trendy new restaurant, and without any advertising, it soon booked the fourth-floor banquet space every weekend in December for private Christmas parties.

The next year brought a steady stream of business, as patrons of the Peace Center flocked to the 858 to get a sophisticated meal before or after seeing a show. In the summer, a test run was made for hosting a disco night in the fourth-floor banquet room. It was overrun with people, so it was quickly turned into a weekly event called Funky Friday.

Chef Grosshans' menu was eclectic. Guests could enjoy such diverse flavors as Asian, Southwestern, Italian and traditional American. Appetizers ranged from chicken cilantro spring rolls, chicken quesadillas and beef carpaccio to lump crab cakes, cream of potato-dill soup and a fresh soup du jour. Entrées included crisped soft-shell crab salad, roasted double French breast of free-range chicken, grilled smoked-lamb steak, rib-eye and steamed Manila clams and fettuccini. According to Sobocinski, the most popular entrée was the potato-crusted grouper served over celery mashed potatoes with haricots verts and tomatoes, maple cream corn and topped off with roasted shallot sour cream.

Perhaps the most revolutionary aspect that the 858 contributed to the emerging modern culinary scene was the presentation of the food itself. The traditional way that Greenvillians saw food presented at local restaurants was classically laid out with a meat/protein at the front and vegetables or starches in quadrants around the plate. What Chef Grosshans introduced was food that stacked in an aesthetically pleasing way, with the vegetables and starches on the bottom and the protein layered on top with sauces creatively drizzled or spooned over the top and around the plate's perimeter.

Above: Exterior of the Elks Lodge No. 858 building. *Courtesy of the Greenville County Historical Society.*

Opposite, inset: The 858 Restaurant's art deco–style logo. *Courtesy of Carl Sobocinski.*

The year 1995 was one of big expansion for the restaurant owners. Downtown Brewing Co. opened on the first floor of the building in October 1995. This venture was a pioneering effort for what would become a hugely popular craft brewery scene. In the same year, a $1 million restaurant called Frescoes was opened in the newly renovated Greenville Mall, and the Downtown Dining Group was created as the identity of the growing list of restaurants. That same year, city councilman Knox White was elected as the new mayor of Greenville and soon began an aggressive and strategic revitalization that would make downtown vibrant again.

Unfortunately, the Downtown Brewing Co. and Frescoes restaurants were short-lived, and both closed toward the end of 1996. Carl Sobocinski left the partnership that year and soon began work on opening his own concept, Soby's New South Cuisine. With original partners Carl and Larry now gone, King realized that since he was less hands-on with the day-to-day operations, it was best to sell the remaining 858 property. In April 1997, ownership of the 858 was taken over by Kip Wynne, John Kirk and Steve Boone, who were already the owners of Trio—A Brick Oven Cafe and two Portofino locations. The group updated the décor and added seasonal menus. John Kirk was the new manager and co-chef with Crawford Campbell. The new ownership and menu weren't enough to keep the restaurant afloat amid the beginnings of what would become a downtown restaurant boom. When the restaurant opened in 1993, there were just thirty-two eateries in the central business district. By the time the 858 closed in 1998, there were around seventy. The growth and competition of downtown dining options that contributed to the closing of the 858 remains in 2020 and is one of the deciding factors of which restaurants continue to thrive and which become members of the "lost restaurants of Greenville."

Epilogue

A Word About the Present

A report from the U.S. Census Bureau in 2017 ranked Greenville, South Carolina, as the fourth-fastest growing city in America. As a tour guide who interacts with thousands of visitors every year and spends time downtown most days of the week, I can certainly attest to the incredible growth of people, buildings, parks, activities, events and, yes, restaurants in our city. In 2020, approximately 120 restaurants occupy space of one square mile in the central business district of Greenville's downtown. Selecting a place to eat out is either easy (walk to the closest one or pick a favorite) or a bit frustrating (trying to get to all the places you haven't been to yet). It's a good problem to have.

The diversity of cooking styles, ethnic cuisines, price points, atmospheres and food and drink themes contribute to a city that already has a lot to offer. The international makeup of the Greenville area has grown significantly in the last few decades—at times ranking first in the United States for per capita direct investment. Consequently, it is now possible to not only find southern and American fare but also restaurants representing Spanish, Italian, French, German, Dutch, Indian, Thai, Korean, Caribbean, Jamaican, Afghan, Persian, Japanese, Chinese, Moroccan, Mediterranean, Irish, Greek, Mexican and many more cuisines. Plenty of meat-and-threes can still be found in the area, continuing a tradition of food that probably has the deepest Upstate roots.

Main Street's charm continues to attract expansions from notable Charleston restaurants. I already discussed High Cotton and Hall's Chophouse making moves here, but the arrival of one of the Holy City's most famous eateries, Husk, caused a sensation when it opened in 2018 in the heart of Greenville's historic West End. A growing number of other regional markets have found in Greenville an attractive place to grow their concepts. Tupelo Honey and Biscuit Head from Asheville have found plenty of loyal patrons here. Charlotte, Raleigh and Knoxville restaurants have also made migrations to our city. While these regional expansions to Greenville are more common, the dominant makeup of places to eat are locally owned and independent restaurants. Few national chains can be found in the downtown core.

Following Chef John Malik's James Beard nomination in 2008, it took ten years for the next appearance of Greenville on the list. In 2018, the foundation recognized Chef Greg McPhee's Anchorage Restaurant as a semifinalist for the Best New Restaurant. Just a year later, in 2019, Husk Greenville's executive chef, Jon Buck, was nominated as a semifinalist for Best Chef Southeast. Greenville has attracted more and more notable chefs to its kitchens, including industry veteran Chef Michael Kramer. Kramer, who opened McCrady's in Charleston and Voice in Houston, came to Greenville in 2013 to be executive chef of culinary operations for

Chef Michael Kramer is a nationally acclaimed chef who worked in top restaurants in Charleston, Houston and other cities before moving to Greenville to be a corporate chef for the Table301 Restaurant Group. *From author's collection.*

Top national chefs come for Euphoria's cooking and panel events. Chef Sean Brock is part of this panel. *Courtesy of Euphoria.*

the Table301 restaurant group. He has since opened Jianna in Greenville as executive chef and partner. Other chefs, like Teryi Youngblood and Tania Harris have received statewide recognition as Chef Ambassadors.

Food festivals and events continue to contribute to the food culture of Greenville. The food truck and cart count in 2019 is at thirty-five, with sporadic Food Truck Rodeo events dotting the calendar. Special theme festivals like Jeff Bannister's Bovinoche create a buzz and spectacle of local and regional chefs coming together to cook a whole cow and other animals. The Southern Exposure food, wine and music event that Carl Sobocinski and Edwin McCain founded was later renamed Euphoria and hosts some of the most sought-after food event tickets in the Southeast. Each year, it brings in nationally acclaimed chefs, winemakers, musicians and a bevy of travel writers who help spread the word of Greenville's culinary scene and charm to the world. Fall for Greenville is Greenville's longest-running food festival (starting in 1982) and draws more than one hundred thousand people to sample scores of Greenville restaurants' food and drinks. Further food and drink options that activate the culinary landscape are the weekend farmer's market events with local craft bakers, outdoor food courts like Gather GVL, in-door communal food courts like

Top: Fall for Greenville is the city's largest annual food festival. *From author's collection.*

Bottom: Many artisan bakers, pop-up restaurants and other specialties have rounded out Greenville's culinary landscape in recent years, like the Fancy Fox Bakeshop. *From author's collection.*

the Commons, farmers and specialty drink makers, as well as food tours, brewery tours and winery tours.

In 2013, John Mariani, a highly respected food and travel writer, wrote an article in *Esquire* titled "Is Greenville the Next Big Food City of the South?" To be in conversations like that is pretty exciting. The present culinary scene of Greenville is vibrant and strong, and the future is promising to only get better.

Bibliography

Greenville News. 1885–2019.

Huff, A.V. *Greenville: The History of the City and County in the South Carolina Piedmont*. Columbia: University of South Carolina Press, 1995.

Janzer, Cinnamon. "The History of the Farm to Table Movement." *Upserve Restaurant Insider*, June 22, 2018.

McKoy, Henry B. *Greenville, S.C. As Seen through the Eyes of Henry Bacon McKoy: Facts and Memories*. Greenville, SC: self-published, 1989.

Nolan, John. *A Guide to Historic Greenville, South Carolina*. Charleston, SC: The History Press, 2008.

Rhew, Adam. "How the Meat and Three Celebrates Southern Bounty: Pick Your Protein, Pick Your Sides, and Grab a Seat at the Table." *Eater*, December 27, 2016.

About the Author

John Nolan has always loved to read about and learn from history. His bachelor of fine arts (Bowling Green State University) and master of arts (Bob Jones University) degrees were both in studio art, but the subject of history was equally enjoyable. The two interests merged perfectly in the job as curator of the Bob Jones University Museum and Gallery, which he held for twenty years. Giving tours and lectures on a world-class collection of master paintings made Nolan realize how much he enjoyed creating memorable learning experiences for the community. While curator, Nolan published six art exhibition catalogs, ranging in topics from Italian Trecento and northern Renaissance painters to Italian Baroque painters and Russian icons.

The sense that something very special was happening in Greenville, South Carolina's downtown revitalization was palpable by the early 2000s. Recognizing that there were no formal tours for the increasing number of city visitors, Nolan joined his passion for tour-giving with the love of his adopted hometown and launched Greenville History Tours in August 2006.

Two years later, Nolan published *A Guide to Historic Greenville, South Carolina* with The History Press and brought the first culinary tour, At the Chef's Table Culinary Tour, to Greenville. Succeeding tours included the Tastes of the South Food Tour, Greenville BBQ Trail Tour, International Coffee Course, and Greenville Breakfast Tour.

On the tenth anniversary of his business, VisitGreenvilleSC honored Nolan with the inaugural Gold Star Ambassador award. Travel writers have featured his tours in the *Boston Globe, Chicago Tribune, New York Post, HuffPost, National Geographic Traveler, Food & Wine, Southern Living, Money* magazine and *Vogue*.

To find more about downtown Greenville walking, driving and culinary tours, contact:

John M. Nolan, owner
Greenville History Tours
Email: greenvillehistorytours@gmail.com
Website: www.greenvillehistorytours.com
Instagram: @greenvillehistorytours
Twitter: @gvilletours
Facebook: https://www.facebook.com/GreenvilleHistoryTours and
   https://www.facebook.com/GreenvilleCulinaryTours

Greenville Restaurant Memories

Greenville Restaurant Memories

Greenville Restaurant Memories

Visit us at
www.historypress.com